THE SIMPSONS™
HOMER FOR THE HOLIDAYS

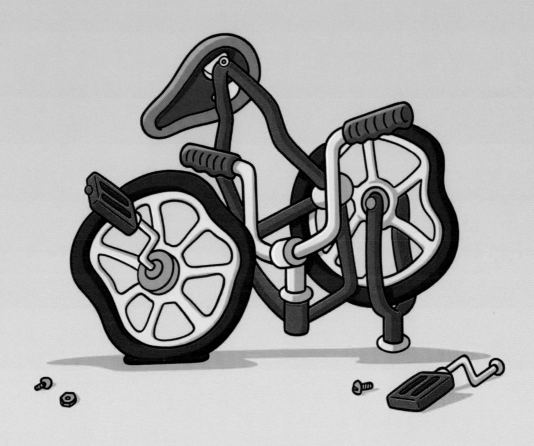

HARPER

NEW YORK · LONDON · TORONTO · SYDNEY

THE SIMPSONS: HOMER FOR THE HOLIDAYS

Copyright © 2006, 2007, 2008 & 2010 by
Bongo Entertainment, Inc. All rights reserved.
No part of this book may be used or reproduced in any manner whatsoever
without written permission except in the case of brief quotations
embodied in critical articles and reviews. For information address
HarperCollins Publishers,
10 East 53rd Street, New York, NY 10022.

FIRST EDITION
ISBN 978-0-06-187673-8

10 11 12 13 14 10 9 8 7 6 5 4 3 2 1

Publisher: Matt Groening
Creative Director: Bill Morrison
Managing Editor: Terry Delegeane
Director of Operations: Robert Zaugh
Art Director: Nathan Kane
Art Director Special Projects: Serban Cristescu
Production Manager: Chris Ungar
Assistant Art Director: Chia-Hsien Jason Ho
Production/Design: Karen Bates, Nathan Hamill, Art Villanueva
Staff Artist: Mike Rote
Administration: Sherri Smith, Pete Benson
Legal Guardian: Susan A. Grode

Trade Paperback Concepts and Design: Serban Cristescu

Cover: Chia-Hsien Jason Ho, Mike Rote, and Serban Cristescu

HarperCollins Editors: Hope Innelli, Jeremy Cesarec

Contributing Artists:
Marcos Asprec, Karen Bates, John Costanza, Serban Cristescu, Dan Davis,
Mike DeCarlo, John Delaney, Mark Ervin, Shane Glines, Nathan Hamill, Chia-Hsien Jason Ho,
Nathan Kane, James Lloyd, Scott McRae, Bill Morrison, Kevin M. Newman, Joey Nilges, Phyllis Novin,
Phil Ortiz, Andrew Pepoy, Jeremy Robinson, Mike Rote, Robert Stanley, Steve Steere Jr.,
Chris Ungar, Carlos Valenti, Art Villanueva, Ken Wheaton

Contributing Writers:
James W. Bates, Tony DiGerolamo, Paul Dini, Chuck Dixon, Evan Dorkin,
Sarah Dyer, Arie Kaplan, Misty Lee, Eric Rogers

Printed in the U.S.A.

CONTENTS

ITEM NO.82295

0 40836 05952 7

100282802

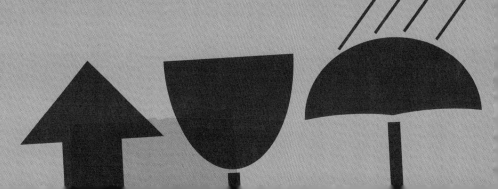

CHRISTMAS EVE
on Evergreen Terrace

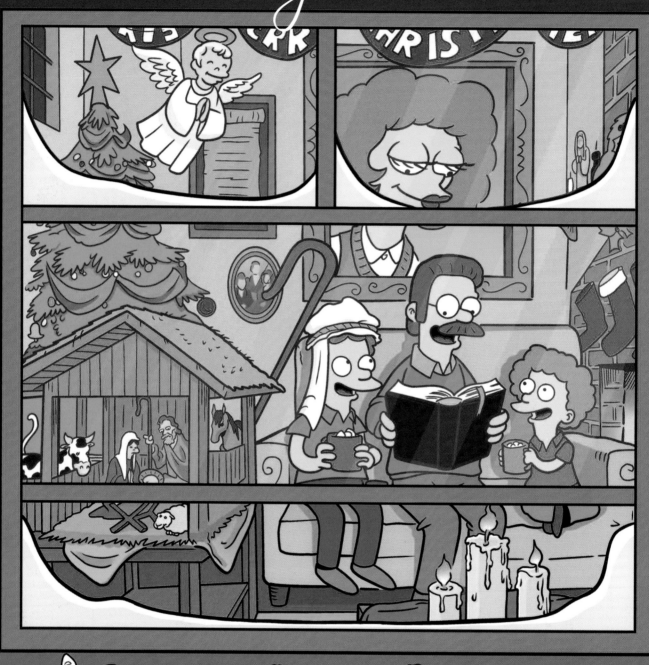

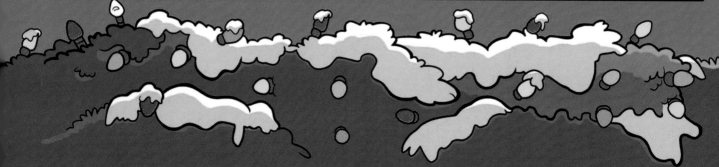

CHRISTM
Homer
HOMER

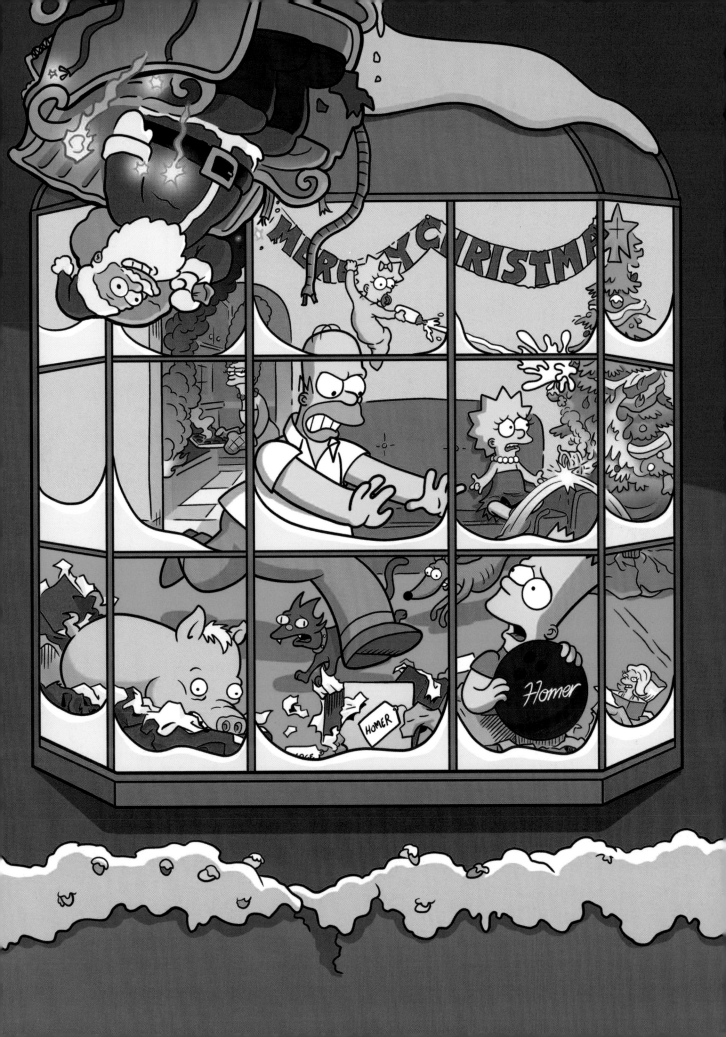

MATT GROENING presents

SPRINGFIELD'S LETTERS TO SANTA

SPRINGFIELD'S LETTERS TO SANTA
SANTA? SANTA!
WHERE IS THAT MAN?
SANTA'S WORKSHOP
NORTH POLE

PAUL DINI SCRIPT | **PHIL ORTIZ** PENCILS | **MIKE DeCARLO** INKS | **NATHAN HAMILL** COLORS | **KAREN BATES** LETTERS | **BILL MORRISON** EDITOR

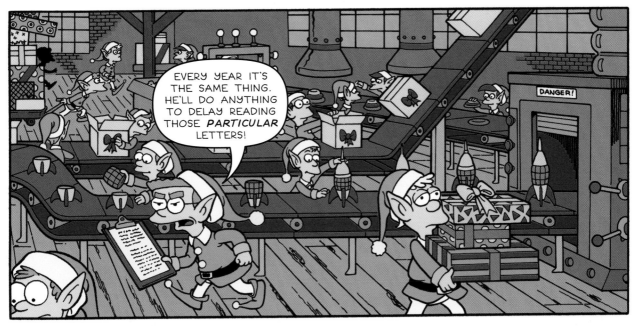

EVERY YEAR IT'S THE SAME THING. HE'LL DO ANYTHING TO DELAY READING THOSE *PARTICULAR* LETTERS!

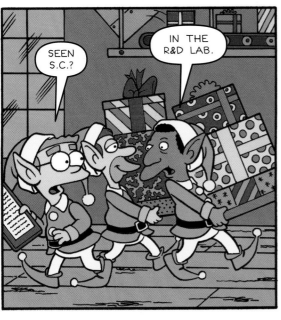

SEEN S.C.?

IN THE R&D LAB.

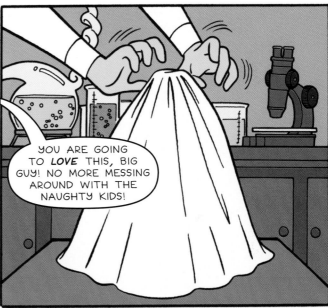

YOU ARE GOING TO *LOVE* THIS, BIG GUY! NO MORE MESSING AROUND WITH THE NAUGHTY KIDS!

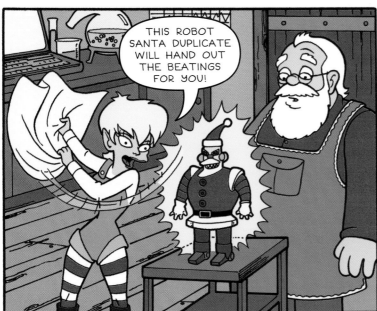

THIS ROBOT SANTA DUPLICATE WILL HAND OUT THE BEATINGS FOR YOU!

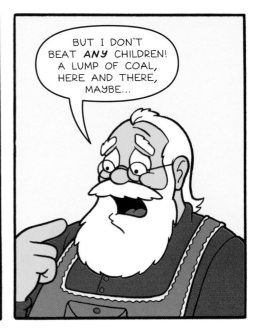

BUT I DON'T BEAT *ANY* CHILDREN! A LUMP OF COAL, HERE AND THERE, MAYBE...

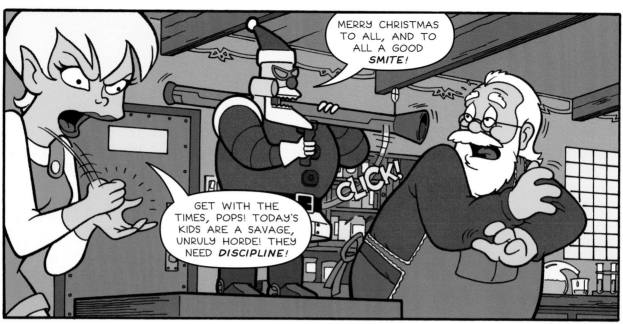

MERRY CHRISTMAS TO ALL, AND TO ALL A GOOD *SMITE!*

CLICK!

GET WITH THE TIMES, POPS! TODAY'S KIDS ARE A SAVAGE, UNRULY HORDE! THEY NEED *DISCIPLINE!*

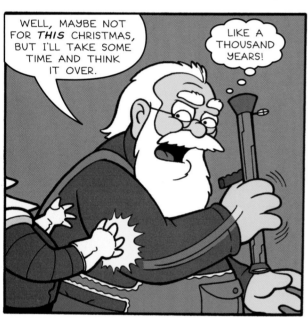

WELL, MAYBE NOT FOR *THIS* CHRISTMAS, BUT I'LL TAKE SOME TIME AND THINK IT OVER.

LIKE A THOUSAND YEARS!

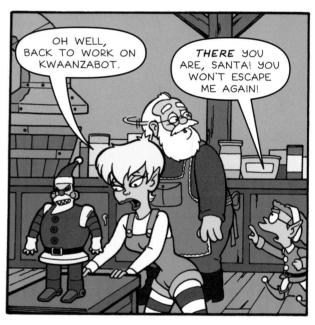

OH WELL, BACK TO WORK ON KWAANZABOT.

THERE YOU ARE, SANTA! YOU WON'T ESCAPE ME AGAIN!

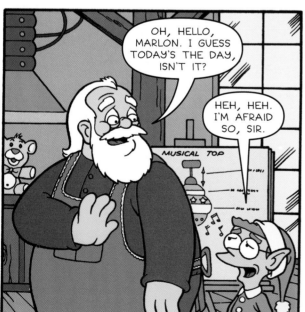

OH, HELLO, MARLON. I GUESS TODAY'S THE DAY, ISN'T IT?

HEH, HEH. I'M AFRAID SO, SIR.

MUSICAL TOP

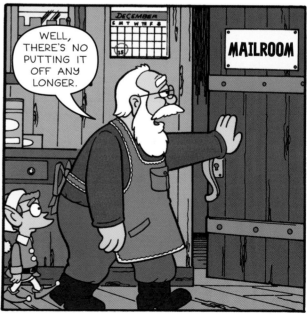

WELL, THERE'S NO PUTTING IT OFF ANY LONGER.

DECEMBER

MAILROOM

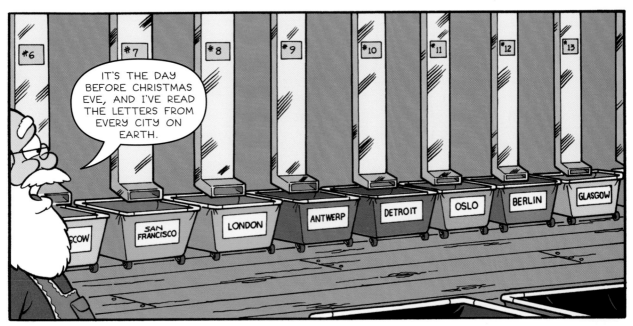

IT'S THE DAY BEFORE CHRISTMAS EVE, AND I'VE READ THE LETTERS FROM EVERY CITY ON EARTH.

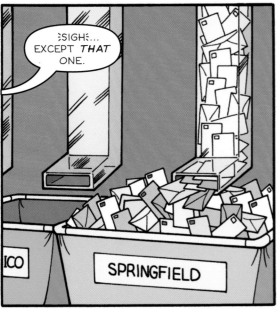

:SIGH:... EXCEPT *THAT* ONE.

SPRINGFIELD

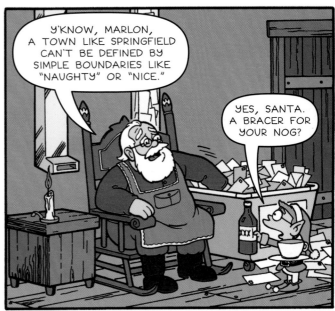

Y'KNOW, MARLON, A TOWN LIKE SPRINGFIELD CAN'T BE DEFINED BY SIMPLE BOUNDARIES LIKE "NAUGHTY" OR "NICE."

YES, SANTA. A BRACER FOR YOUR NOG?

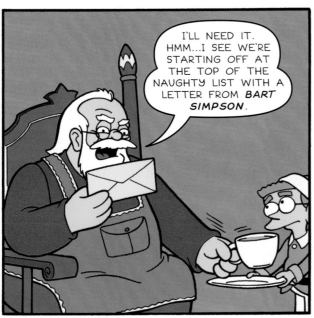

I'LL NEED IT. HMM...I SEE WE'RE STARTING OFF AT THE TOP OF THE NAUGHTY LIST WITH A LETTER FROM *BART SIMPSON*.

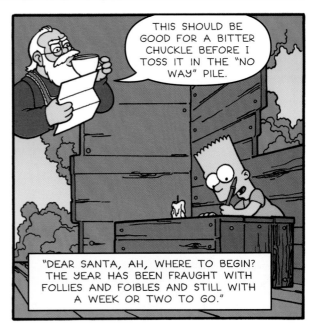

THIS SHOULD BE GOOD FOR A BITTER CHUCKLE BEFORE I TOSS IT IN THE "NO WAY" PILE.

"DEAR SANTA, AH, WHERE TO BEGIN? THE YEAR HAS BEEN FRAUGHT WITH FOLLIES AND FOIBLES AND STILL WITH A WEEK OR TWO TO GO."

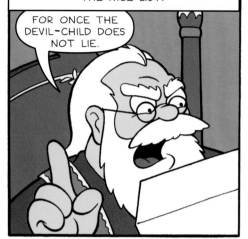

"I SUPPOSE IF YOU'VE BEEN KEEPING WATCH ON ME THE LAST TWELVE MONTHS, YOU KNOW I DON'T STAND A SNOWBALL'S CHANCE IN H-E-DOUBLE HOCKEY STICKS OF MAKING THE NICE LIST."

FOR ONCE THE DEVIL-CHILD DOES NOT LIE.

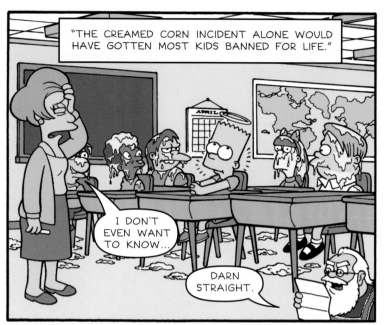

"THE CREAMED CORN INCIDENT ALONE WOULD HAVE GOTTEN MOST KIDS BANNED FOR LIFE."

I DON'T EVEN WANT TO KNOW...

DARN STRAIGHT.

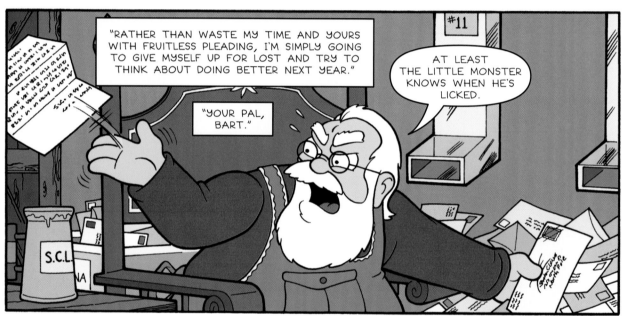

"RATHER THAN WASTE MY TIME AND YOURS WITH FRUITLESS PLEADING, I'M SIMPLY GOING TO GIVE MYSELF UP FOR LOST AND TRY TO THINK ABOUT DOING BETTER NEXT YEAR."

"YOUR PAL, BART."

AT LEAST THE LITTLE MONSTER KNOWS WHEN HE'S LICKED.

S.C.L.
NA

#11

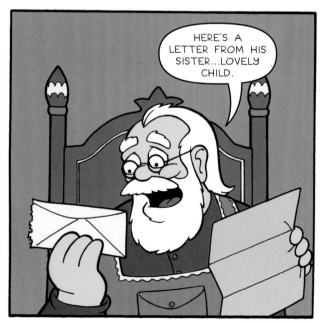

HERE'S A LETTER FROM HIS SISTER...LOVELY CHILD.

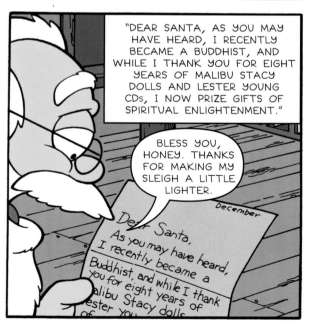

"DEAR SANTA, AS YOU MAY HAVE HEARD, I RECENTLY BECAME A BUDDHIST, AND WHILE I THANK YOU FOR EIGHT YEARS OF MALIBU STACY DOLLS AND LESTER YOUNG CDs, I NOW PRIZE GIFTS OF SPIRITUAL ENLIGHTENMENT."

BLESS YOU, HONEY. THANKS FOR MAKING MY SLEIGH A LITTLE LIGHTER.

December

Dear Santa,
As you may have heard,
I recently became a
Buddhist, and while I thank
you for eight years of
Malibu Stacy dolls
Lester You

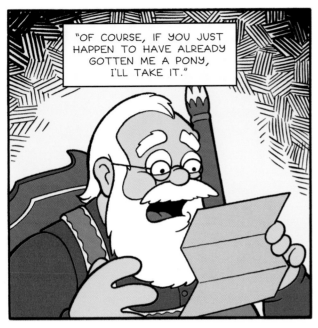

"OF COURSE, IF YOU JUST HAPPEN TO HAVE ALREADY GOTTEN ME A PONY, I'LL TAKE IT."

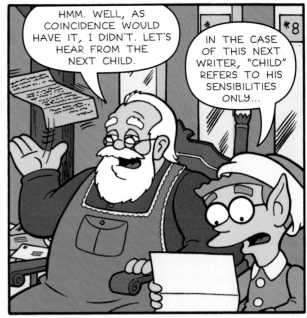

HMM. WELL, AS COINCIDENCE WOULD HAVE IT, I DIDN'T. LET'S HEAR FROM THE NEXT CHILD.

IN THE CASE OF THIS NEXT WRITER, "CHILD" REFERS TO HIS SENSIBILITIES ONLY...

#8

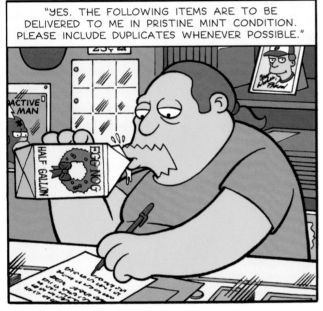

"YES. THE FOLLOWING ITEMS ARE TO BE DELIVERED TO ME IN PRISTINE MINT CONDITION. PLEASE INCLUDE DUPLICATES WHENEVER POSSIBLE."

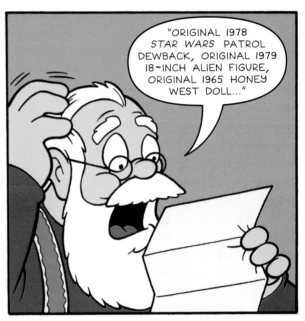

"ORIGINAL 1978 STAR WARS PATROL DEWBACK, ORIGINAL 1979 18-INCH ALIEN FIGURE, ORIGINAL 1965 HONEY WEST DOLL..."

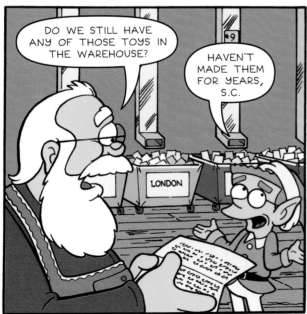

DO WE STILL HAVE ANY OF THOSE TOYS IN THE WAREHOUSE?

HAVEN'T MADE THEM FOR YEARS, S.C.

LONDON

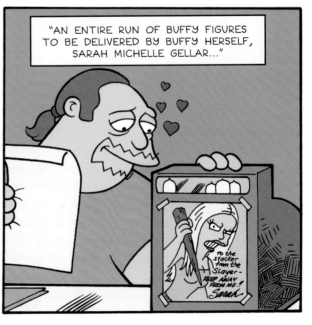

"AN ENTIRE RUN OF BUFFY FIGURES TO BE DELIVERED BY BUFFY HERSELF, SARAH MICHELLE GELLAR..."

TO THE STALKER FROM THE SLAYER- KEEP AWAY FROM ME! Sarah

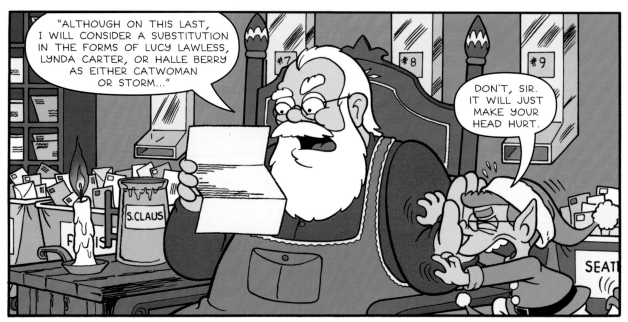

"ALTHOUGH ON THIS LAST, I WILL CONSIDER A SUBSTITUTION IN THE FORMS OF LUCY LAWLESS, LYNDA CARTER, OR HALLE BERRY AS EITHER CATWOMAN OR STORM..."

DON'T, SIR. IT WILL JUST MAKE YOUR HEAD HURT.

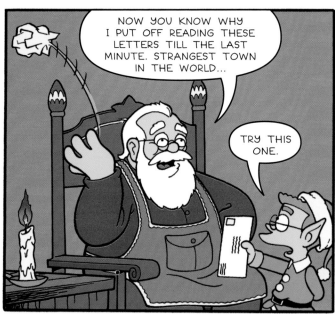

NOW YOU KNOW WHY I PUT OFF READING THESE LETTERS TILL THE LAST MINUTE. STRANGEST TOWN IN THE WORLD...

TRY THIS ONE.

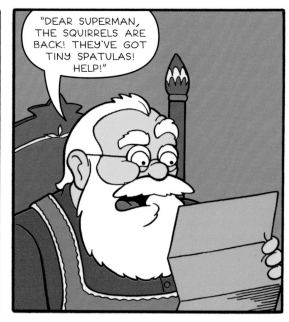

"DEAR SUPERMAN, THE SQUIRRELS ARE BACK! THEY'VE GOT TINY SPATULAS! HELP!"

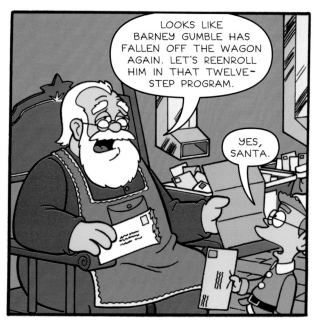

LOOKS LIKE BARNEY GUMBLE HAS FALLEN OFF THE WAGON AGAIN. LET'S REENROLL HIM IN THAT TWELVE-STEP PROGRAM.

YES, SANTA.

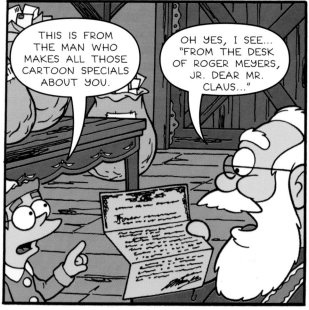

THIS IS FROM THE MAN WHO MAKES ALL THOSE CARTOON SPECIALS ABOUT YOU.

OH YES, I SEE... "FROM THE DESK OF ROGER MEYERS, JR. DEAR MR. CLAUS..."

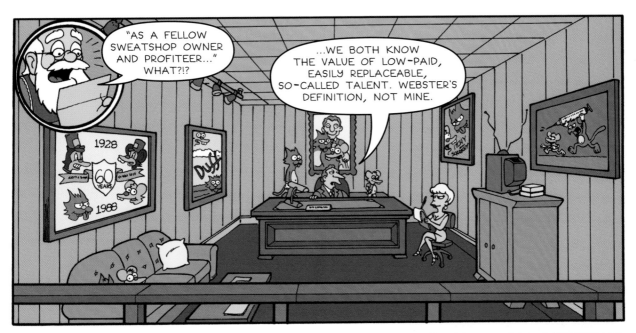

"AS A FELLOW SWEATSHOP OWNER AND PROFITEER..." WHAT?!?

...WE BOTH KNOW THE VALUE OF LOW-PAID, EASILY REPLACEABLE, SO-CALLED TALENT. WEBSTER'S DEFINITION, NOT MINE.

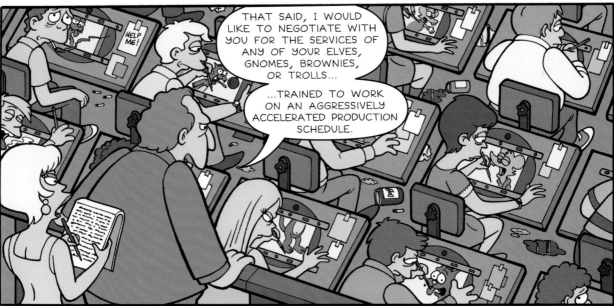

THAT SAID, I WOULD LIKE TO NEGOTIATE WITH YOU FOR THE SERVICES OF ANY OF YOUR ELVES, GNOMES, BROWNIES, OR TROLLS...

...TRAINED TO WORK ON AN AGGRESSIVELY ACCELERATED PRODUCTION SCHEDULE.

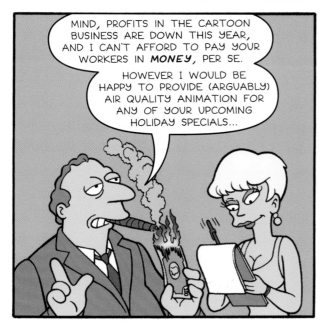

MIND, PROFITS IN THE CARTOON BUSINESS ARE DOWN THIS YEAR, AND I CAN'T AFFORD TO PAY YOUR WORKERS IN *MONEY*, PER SE.

HOWEVER I WOULD BE HAPPY TO PROVIDE (ARGUABLY) AIR QUALITY ANIMATION FOR ANY OF YOUR UPCOMING HOLIDAY SPECIALS...

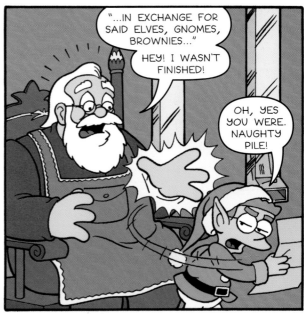

"...IN EXCHANGE FOR SAID ELVES, GNOMES, BROWNIES..."

HEY! I WASN'T FINISHED!

OH, YES YOU WERE. NAUGHTY PILE!

JUST ONCE I'D LIKE TO GET A LETTER FROM ANYONE IN THAT TOWN WHO THINKS ABOUT THEIR FELLOW MAN.
GOTCHA COVERED, BIG GUY. THIS ONE'S FROM NED FLANDERS.
"DEAR SANTA, AT THIS BLESS-I-DIDDLY TIME OF THE YEAR, IT IS BETTER TO GIVE THAN TO RECEIVE."
AH, GOOD OLD NED. AT LEAST **HE** HASN'T FORGOTTEN THE TRUE MEANING OF CHRISTMAS.
"SO I THINK YOU SHOULD GIVE EVERY-DIDDLY-THING YOU WOULD GIVE-I-DIDDLY TO ME TO MY BEST-I-DIDDLY FRIEND, HOMER SIMPSON. DIDDLY."
I ♥ LEFT-HANDERS
"LOVE, STUPID FLANDERS"?!
THIS IS FROM ***HOMER SIMPSON***!
THAT ***DOES*** IT! I'M GOING TO GO THROUGH EACH AND EVERY LETTER, AND IF THEY ARE ALL AS GREEDY AND AS SELF-SERVING AS THE OTHERS, I'M GOING TO CROSS SPRINGFIELD OFF MY ROUTE ***FOREVER***!
GASP!

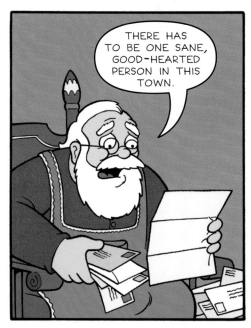

THERE HAS TO BE ONE SANE, GOOD-HEARTED PERSON IN THIS TOWN.

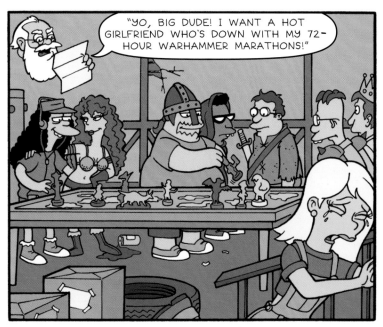

"YO, BIG DUDE! I WANT A HOT GIRLFRIEND WHO'S DOWN WITH MY 72-HOUR WARHAMMER MARATHONS!"

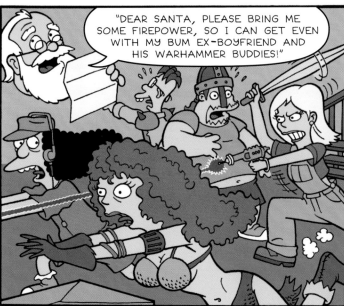

"DEAR SANTA, PLEASE BRING ME SOME FIREPOWER, SO I CAN GET EVEN WITH MY BUM EX-BOYFRIEND AND HIS WARHAMMER BUDDIES!"

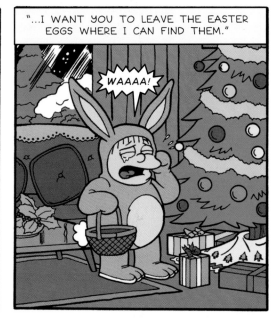

"...I WANT YOU TO LEAVE THE EASTER EGGS WHERE I CAN FIND THEM."

WAAAA!

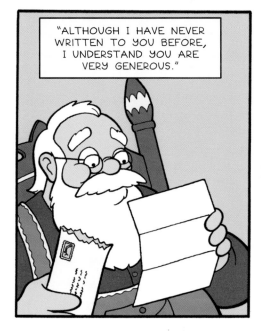

"ALTHOUGH I HAVE NEVER WRITTEN TO YOU BEFORE, I UNDERSTAND YOU ARE VERY GENEROUS."

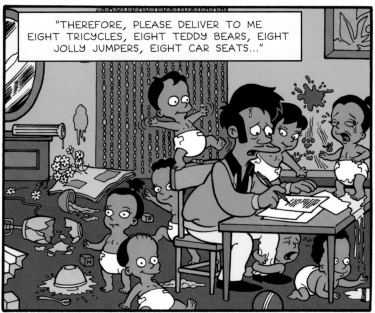

"THEREFORE, PLEASE DELIVER TO ME EIGHT TRICYCLES, EIGHT TEDDY BEARS, EIGHT JOLLY JUMPERS, EIGHT CAR SEATS..."

I WANT WHAT SHERRI'S GETTING, ONLY BETTER.
I WANT WHAT TERRI'S GETTING, ONLY BETTER.
"...MY OWN SLEIGH AND REINDEER, FOR FAST GETAWAYS."
CLUB
FOUNDED 1937
"...MY OWN SLEIGH AND REINDEER, FOR FAST GETAWAYS."
"...MY OWN SLEIGH AND REINDEER, FOR FAST GETAWAYS."
...THE RETURN OF THE BULL MOOSE PARTY.
...AN ASSORTMENT OF CHEMICAL EXPLOSIVES AND THAT NEW RECORDING OF RUDDIGORE I'VE BEEN READING ABOUT IN *THE GRAMOPHONE*.
GLAAH-HAA! *CATS!*
...A REASON TO LIVE THROUGH THE HOLIDAYS. ANY REASON. I AIN'T PICKY.

ENOUGH! I'VE MADE MY DECISION!
#100
FROM THIS MOMENT ON, THE TOWN OF SPRINGFIELD IS--
THERE'S STILL ONE MORE LETTER LEFT, S.C.
"DEAR SANTA, I DOUBT YOU STILL REMEMBER ME OR THAT STRANGE CHRISTMAS YOU, ME, AND MONTY BURNS SHARED BACK IN '44."
I REMEMBER. I STILL HAVE THAT LUMP FROM WHEN BURNS WHACKED ME WITH A COCONUT.
"IT'S FUNNY, BUT I CAN'T REMEMBER EVER ENJOYING A CHRISTMAS MORE THAN THAT TIME I HELPED YOU GET READY FOR YOUR BIG FLIGHT."
HO, HO. IT WAS UNIQUE, I'LL GIVE HIM THAT.
"I'M AN OLD MAN NOW, SANTA, AND I'M AFRAID I DON'T HAVE MANY CHRISTMASES LEFT."

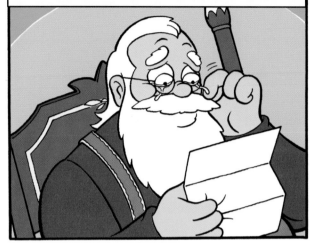

"IF I COULD HAVE ONE LAST CHRISTMAS WISH, IT WOULD BE TO ASSIST YOU AGAIN IN YOUR MISSION TO BRING HAPPINESS TO THE WORLD. DAGNABBIT, FORGET THE WORLD, I'D SETTLE FOR MY OWN LITTLE TOWN OF SPRINGFIELD."

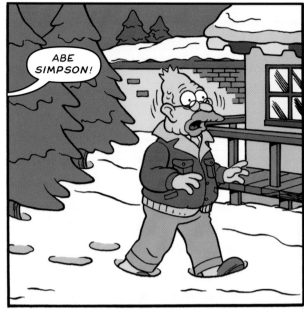

ABE SIMPSON!

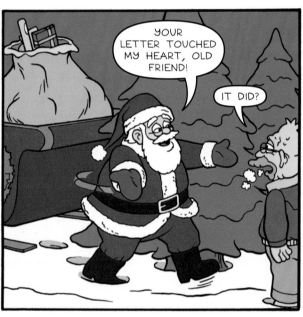

YOUR LETTER TOUCHED MY HEART, OLD FRIEND!

IT DID?

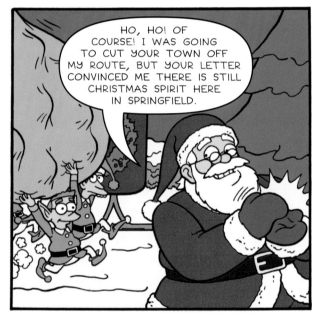

HO, HO! OF COURSE! I WAS GOING TO CUT YOUR TOWN OFF MY ROUTE, BUT YOUR LETTER CONVINCED ME THERE IS STILL CHRISTMAS SPIRIT HERE IN SPRINGFIELD.

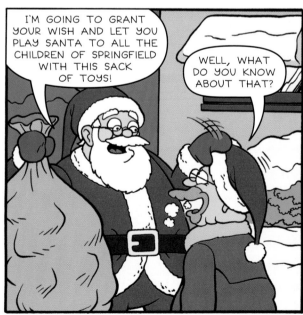

I'M GOING TO GRANT YOUR WISH AND LET YOU PLAY SANTA TO ALL THE CHILDREN OF SPRINGFIELD WITH THIS SACK OF TOYS!

WELL, WHAT DO YOU KNOW ABOUT THAT?

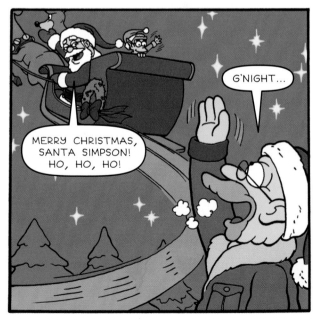

G'NIGHT...

MERRY CHRISTMAS, SANTA SIMPSON! HO, HO, HO!

NOW WHO THE SAM HILL WAS *THAT*?
MR. SIMPSON! WHAT ARE YOU DOING OUTSIDE IN THE SNOW?!
MY GRANDSON CALLED AND TOLD ME TO WAIT OUT HERE. MY FAMILY'S PICKING ME UP. WE'RE GOING TO GO CAROLING, AND SLEIGH RIDING, AND DRINK HOT CHOCOLATE...
NONSENSE! GET INSIDE THIS INSTANT!
BWA-HA-HA-HA! SUCKER!
FROM THE DESK OF ABE SIMPSON
THE END

NOT A (GREEN, SLIMY) CREATURE WAS STIRRING

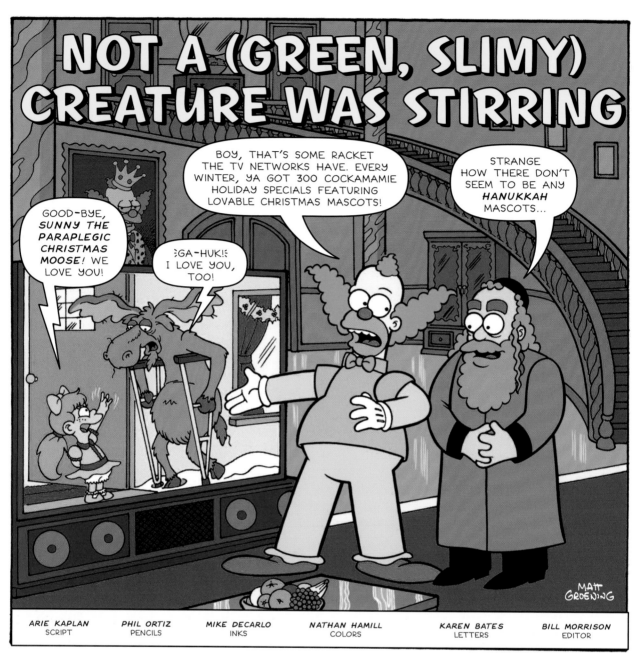

GOOD-BYE, **SUNNY THE PARAPLEGIC CHRISTMAS MOOSE!** WE LOVE YOU!

EGA-HUK! I LOVE YOU, TOO!

BOY, THAT'S SOME RACKET THE TV NETWORKS HAVE. EVERY WINTER, YA GOT 300 COCKAMAMIE HOLIDAY SPECIALS FEATURING LOVABLE CHRISTMAS MASCOTS!

STRANGE HOW THERE DON'T SEEM TO BE ANY *HANUKKAH* MASCOTS...

| ARIE KAPLAN | PHIL ORTIZ | MIKE DECARLO | NATHAN HAMILL | KAREN BATES | BILL MORRISON |
| SCRIPT | PENCILS | INKS | COLORS | LETTERS | EDITOR |

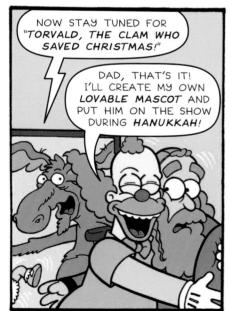

NOW STAY TUNED FOR *"TORVALD, THE CLAM WHO SAVED CHRISTMAS!"*

DAD, THAT'S IT! I'LL CREATE MY OWN *LOVABLE MASCOT* AND PUT HIM ON THE SHOW DURING *HANUKKAH!*

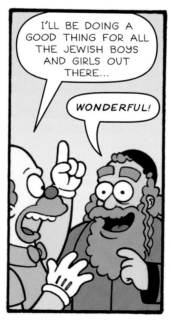

I'LL BE DOING A GOOD THING FOR ALL THE JEWISH BOYS AND GIRLS OUT THERE...

WONDERFUL!

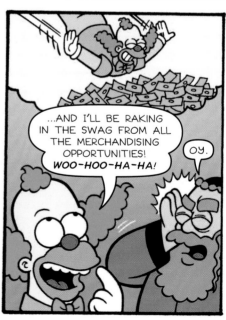

...AND I'LL BE RAKING IN THE SWAG FROM ALL THE MERCHANDISING OPPORTUNITIES! *WOO-HOO-HA-HA!*

OY.

THE VERY NEXT DAY...
OKAY, TEAM KRUSTY, I CAME UP WITH TWO DESIGNS FOR MY NEW MASCOT. I NEED TO KNOW WHICH ONE YOU LIKE BEST!
THE FIRST ONE IS CALLED "CHRISTIAN THE KOSHER HANUKKAH PIG" AND THIS OTHER ONE IS "DAMIAN THE PIOUS HANUKKAH LOBSTER" ...WHADDAYA THINK?
COME ON, YES-MEN! GET TO YESSING! WHY AREN'T YOU TELLING ME HOW GREAT MY IDEAS ARE?
KRUSTY, YOUR DRAWINGS... STIR UP EMOTIONS I DIDN'T KNOW I HAD. BUT THEY, UH...LACK SOMETHING...
IS IT SHRIMP? BECAUSE I GOT ANOTHER ONE, "SHLOMO THE HANUKKAH SHRIMP."
NO, THEY LACK...ER, A CHILD'S TOUCH!
A **CHILD'S** TOUCH, EH?
HEY, I **GOT** IT! I'LL BRING IN SOME ACTUAL **CHILDREN** TO DESIGN THE MASCOT FOR ME!

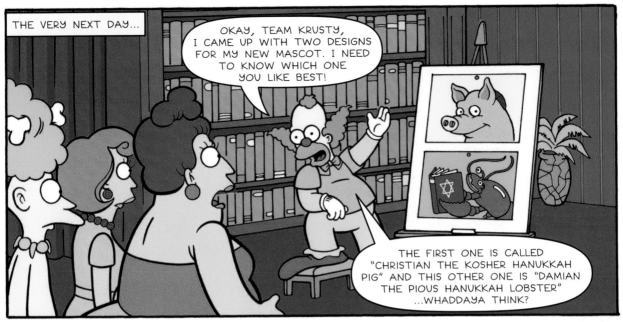

NOW, YOU KIDS HAVE BEEN SELECTED BECAUSE YOU REPRESENT VARIOUS DEMOGRAPHICS...
"BAD BOY."
"ALPHA MALE."
"BRAIN."
"DORK."
I'M DIGGING FOR GOLD IN MY FACE!
"AVERAGE TV VIEWER."
NOW, GO AND MAKE ME A HANUKKAH MASCOT!
YAYYYY!
BRAINSTORMING, STAGE ONE
...AND I SAY THAT THE MASCOT SHOULD BE A MOOSE!
MY FAVORITE MOOSE IS CHOCOLATE!
BUT...OW!... THERE'S ALREADY A CHRISTMAS MOOSE!
I CAN'T HEAR YOU OVER THE SOUND OF YOU HITTING YOURSELF!

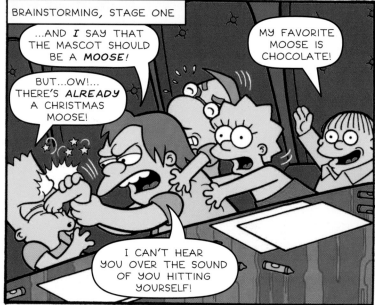

BRAINSTORMING, STAGE TWO
WHY DON'T WE MAKE THE MASCOT A MANTA RAY?
OR A PEGASUS?
OR A STAPLER?
I SAY WE MAKE THE MASCOT A TURTLE.
TURTLES? EWW! WE JUST READ ABOUT THEM IN SCIENCE CLASS. THEY MOULT THEIR DEAD SKIN! IT LOOKS LIKE THIN SHEETS OF PLASTIC, BUT IT'S REALLY :SHUDDER: PIECES OF TURTLE!
COOL!
GENTLEMEN, I REST MY CASE.
BRAINSTORMING, STAGE THREE
NO, BART, WE CAN'T CALL HIM "POOPFACE, THE POOPING TURTLE THAT POOPS EVERYWHERE AND SMELLS HIS OWN POOP."
STUPID FCC REGULATIONS.
THE TURTLE'S FLIPPERS HAVE THREE FINGERS, AND MY FLIPPERS HAVE FOUR FINGERS!
RALPH, THAT'S IT!

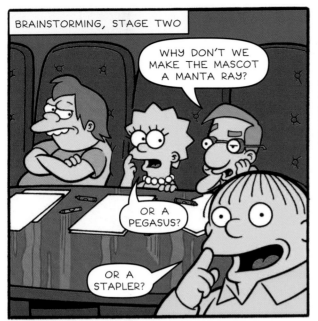

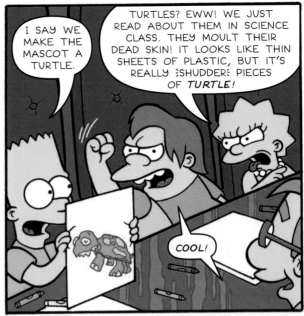

WE'LL CALL HIM FLIPPER THE TURTLE! ALL IN FAVOR?
AYE!
GREAT WORK, RALPH!
I'M A MEDIA SPIN DOCTOR!
...WE CALL IT FLIPPER, THE HANUKKAH TURTLE!
YECCH. LOOKS WEIRD. BUT...YOU'RE KIDS, AND KIDS MUST KNOW WHAT OTHER KIDS WANT TO SEE.
I THINK WE HAVE A WINNER! HAVE THE ART DEPARTMENT MAKE A TURTLE COSTUME, STAT!
YAY!! WE CREATED KRUSTY'S MASCOT!
PLEASE SIGN THIS FORM SAYING YOU DID NOT CREATE KRUSTY'S MASCOT.
CONTRACT

AND SO...
THIS MOSES SKETCH STINKS! WHY CAN'T MY WRITERS STEAL FROM ANY **GOOD** COMEDIANS? GOOD THING WE'VE GOT FLIPPER THE HANUKKAH TURTLE!
ER,...ABOUT THAT, KRUSTY...
SCRIPT
...**THIS** IS WHAT THE COSTUME DEPARTMENT CAME UP WITH.
WHAT?! SIDESHOW MEL, YOU CAN'T GO OUT ON STAGE DRESSED AS **THAT!** IT LOOKS LIKE MILTON BERLE PUKED ON KERMIT THE FROG!
YOU'RE TELLING ME...!
HOW COULD YOU MAKE SUCH AN UGLY COSTUME?
WE JUST FOLLOWED THE DESIGN SKETCH YOU GAVE US.
DESIGN SKETCH? IT WAS DRAWN UP BY A ***TEN-YEAR-OLD!***
WELL, KRUSTY, WHAT SHOULD I DO?
JUST GIMME A MINUTE, AND I'LL THINK OF A WAY TO...
...STALL EVERYONE--
WHOOOAAA!
FLUMP!

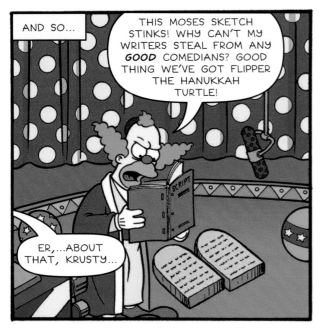

YAAGGGHHH!
EXIT
FEAR NOT, CHILDREN! I AM YOUR LOVABLE BOSOM PAL, FLIPPER THE HANUKKAH TURTLE!
GOOD LORD! ⁝CHOKE!⁝ IT'S A MONSTER!
IF YOU LOOK AT IT, IT'LL STEAL YOUR SOUL!
I CREATED IT, AND IT FREAKS ME OUT!
HAW HAW! I'M SCARRED FOR LIFE!
KRUSTYLU STUDIOS
MY PANTS ARE WETTING THEMSELVES!
OH, THIS AIN'T GOOD.
IN THE PAST HOUR, YOU'VE RECEIVED SEVEN HUNDRED THOUSAND EMAILED DEATH THREATS, SUBPOENAS FROM BOTH KERMIT THE FROG'S LEGAL TEAM AND THE ESTATE OF MILTON BERLE, AND A DISEMBODIED TURTLE'S HEAD WAS FOUND IN YOUR BED.
OH, NO! WHAT DO I DO?!
STRAWBERRY DOWNWARD SPIRAL
COOKIES and DEPRESSION
YOU NEED TO FIND ANOTHER MASCOT...QUICK!

FEAR NOT, CHILDREN! I AM YOUR **LOVABLE BOSOM PAL,** FLIPPER THE HANUKKAH TURTLE!
KODOS! PUT DOWN THAT RIDICULOUS CANCER CURE AND GET OVER HERE! THIS IS ***IMPORTANT!***
IS IT...? COULD IT BE?!?
YES! IT IS ***XARTHON 9,*** THE MIGHTY DEITY OF OUR WINTER SOLSTICE FESTIVAL.
AND HE LOOKS LIKE HE HAS LOST WEIGHT!
BUT WHAT IS THE GREAT AND POWERFUL XARTHON 9 DOING ON EARTH?
I DO NOT KNOW, BUT WE NEED TO JOURNEY THERE TO GREET HIM AND OFFER UP A ***TRIBUTE!*** SOMETHING CLASSY!
AGREED. FETCH THE BLENDER WE RECEIVED LAST ***PON FARR DAY!***

HELP! MY ZIPPER IS STUCK! I'VE BEEN IN THIS COSTUME FOR THREE HOURS, AND I'M STARTING TO SMELL LIKE RANCID PROVOLONE! HELLO? ANYBODY?
WHERE IN THE NAME OF MCGRUFF THE CRIME DOG ARE WE GOING TO FIND ANOTHER ADORABLE MASCOT? IT'S NOT LIKE SOME EASILY MERCHANDISABLE CREATURE IS JUST GOING TO MAGICALLY APPEAR...
FREAKISH MONSTERS? I THOUGHT I'D STOPPED SEEING THOSE ONCE THE '60S ENDED!
FOOLISH HUMAN, YOU SHALL TAKE US TO SEE XARTHON 9!
TAKE YOU TO SEE WHATZIS THE WHO NOW?
THERE HE IS!! *XARTHON 9!*
WE WORSHIP YOU, O XARTHON 9! PLEASE ACCEPT THIS BLENDER FOR ALL YOUR ZORG PROCESSING NEEDS!
WE WILL DO WHATEVER YOU WISH, O MASTER!
UH...
HMMM...THEY'LL DO *ANYTHING* HE SAYS, EH? THAT GIVES ME AN IDEA...
KRUST STUDIO

AND SO, ON THE SECOND NIGHT OF HANUKKAH...
HEY, KIDS! NOW I'VE GOT TWO NEW HANUKKAH MASCOTS ON MY SHOW...

...MOISHE AND MENDEL!
AND THEY'RE NOT HALF AS REVOLTING AS FLIPPER WAS!
BUT KODOS, WHY WOULD OUR DEITY DEMAND THAT WE DEMEAN OURSELVES IN THIS FASHION?
OY GEVALT, KANG! ENOUGH WITH THE COMPLAINING! I'M GOING TO PLOTZ FROM ALL THE TSURIS YOU'RE GIVING ME OVER HERE!
MOISHE
MENDEL
THE END

Here We
CIDER
JOIN US AS WE MAKE OUR ROUNDS SINGING HOLIDAY CLASSICS WITH NEW AND, DARE I SAY, IMPROVED SCI-FI LYRICS!
CHRISTMAS, THE NEW FRONTIER
(TO THE TUNE OF "THE CHRISTMAS SONG")
PHASERS BLASTING NOW IN OPEN FIRE.
KIRK IS SCREAMING AT THE CREW.
KLINGON WAR CHANTS BEING YELLED IN DEFIANCE.
TRIBBLES ARE MATING IN MY SHOE.
EVERYBODY KNOWS THAT SCOTTY ALWAYS DRINKS TOO MUCH.
CHEKOV'S PUNCHING OUT SULU.
SPOCK'S HAD IT WITH THIS ILLOGICAL MESS –
STAR TREK CHRISTMAS...P.U.!

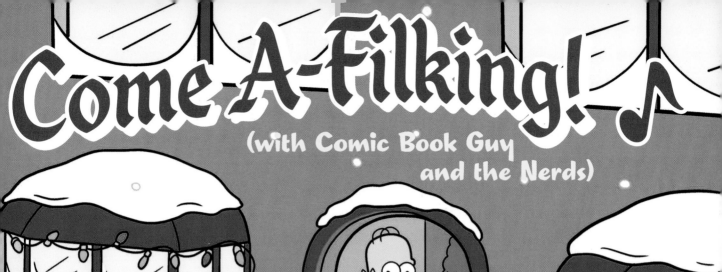

Come A-Filking! ♪

(with Comic Book Guy and the Nerds)

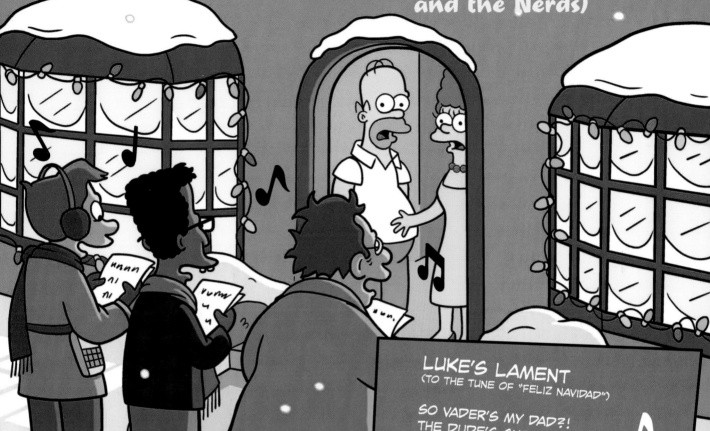

GEEKS IN LINE
(TO THE TUNE OF "SILVER BELLS")

COLOR COVERS, PRETTY COVERS,
WRAPPED IN THIN MYLAR SLEEVES.
OVER THERE, THAT'S AN ISSUE OF
SANDMAN,
NERDS ARE BROWSING, THEY'RE
ESPOUSING
THEORIES ON JUSTICE LEAGUE.
UP AND DOWN EVERY AISLE
YOU'LL SEE:

GEEKS IN LINE, GEEKS IN LINE.
IT'S SHOPPING TIME AT THE DUNGEON.
CHING-A-LING, CASH THEY BRING.
SOON MY LUNCH BILL I CAN PAY!

LUKE'S LAMENT
(TO THE TUNE OF "FELIZ NAVIDAD")

SO VADER'S MY DAD?!
THE DUDE'S SUPERBAD.
HE'S COVERED IN SCARS,
BLOWS UP PLANETS AND STARS,
AND HE CUT OFF MY HAND!

SO LEIA'S MY SIS?!
I CAN'T BELIEVE THIS!
I WISH GEORGE SAID SO,
BUT HE LET US GO
SHARE A PASSIONATE KISS.

I WANNA WISH FOR A MAJOR REWRITE
I WANNA WISH FOR A MAJOR REWRITE
I WANNA WISH FOR A MAJOR REWRITE
TO THIS SILLY SCI-FI SCRIPT!

SO HAN GETS THE GIRL?!
WE'RE IN EWOK-WORLD,
I'M ALONE (OF COURSE),
EXCEPT FOR THE FORCE.
MAN, I JUST WANT TO HURL!

I WANNA WISH FOR A MAJOR REWRITE
I WANNA WISH FOR A MAJOR REWRITE
I WANNA WISH FOR A MAJOR REWRITE
TO THIS SILLY SCI-FI SCRIPT!

BART SIMPSON in BRAVE BART

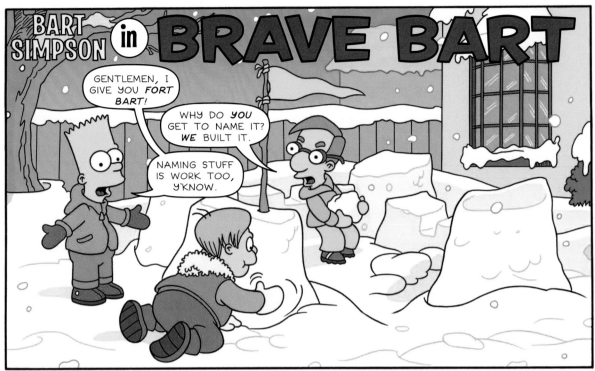

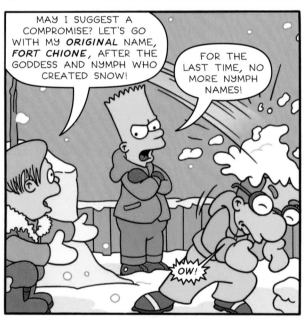

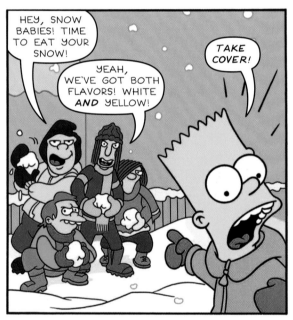

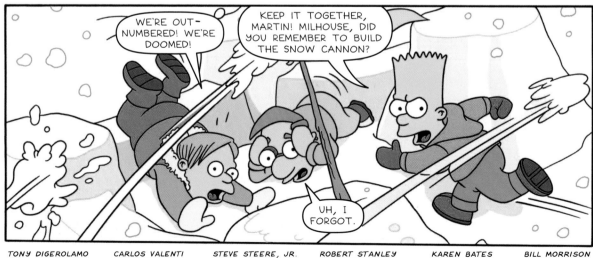

TONY DIGEROLAMO
SCRIPT

CARLOS VALENTI
PENCILS

STEVE STEERE, JR.
INKS

ROBERT STANLEY
COLORS

KAREN BATES
LETTERS

BILL MORRISON
EDITOR

RAAWRR?!
OKAY, WE'RE OUTNUMBERED AND OUTGUNNED, BUT WITH THIS FORT, WE'RE TACTICALLY SUPERIOR. SO ON PAPER, WE'RE *TOTALLY* KICKING BUTT.
I SAY WE SURRENDER. MAYBE THEY'LL HAVE MERCY AND MAKE THEIR WEDGIES QUICK.
LET'S RUN FOR IT.
NO! I'VE GOT IT! WE'LL *ATTACK!*
SPLOOSH!
I AM BART SIMPSON. AND I SEE A WHOLE ARMY OF MY FRIENDS HERE TO FIGHT BULLIES AS FREE MEN! FIGHT, AND WE MAY EAT SNOW. RUN, AND WE MAY NOT EAT SNOW FOR A WHILE. BUT LYING IN YOUR BED DAYS FROM NOW, YOU'LL WILLINGLY TRADE ALL THOSE DAYS TO COME BACK HERE AND TELL THOSE BULLIES, "YOU MAY MAKE US EAT SNOW, BUT YOU WILL NEVER MAKE US EAT *OUR FREEDOM*!"
BART! YOU'RE TALKING CRAZY!
UH, GUYS? THE CHARGE IS STARTING.
GUYS?
WAY TO LEAD A REBELLION, SIMPSON!
YEAH, BUT YOU HAVE TO ADMIT, HIS PLAN WAS TACTICALLY SOUND.
BART'S A MILITARY GENIUS! HE'S *EATING SNOW,* JUST LIKE HE PREDICTED!
AND *WE'RE* EATING WARM, CHEWY *FREEDOM*!
THE END

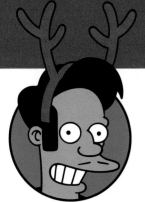

KWIK-E-MART
Holiday Savings Circular

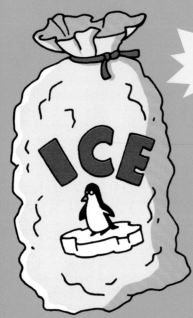

BUY ICE!

It's Seasonal!

LOOK! COVERLESS COMICS

PERFECT WRAPPING PAPER!

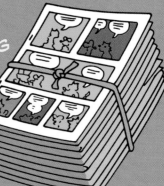

YOUR CHOICE: $12/BUNDLE!

FRESH *ly re-sprinkled* **HOLIDAY DONUTS!**

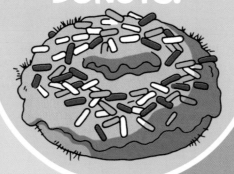

SANTA'S 12-PACK SPECIAL

$AVE!

NEW!

CHRISTMAS *Cherry Squishees!*

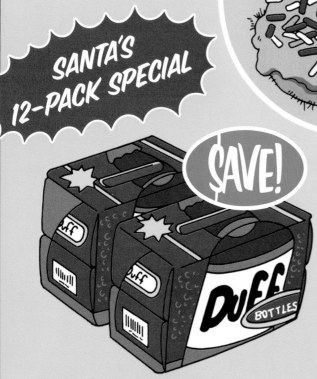

DUFF BOTTLES

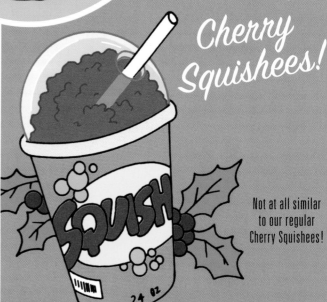

SQUISH

Not at all similar to our regular Cherry Squishees!

BUY 2 CASES OF DUFF BEER, GET 2 MORE AT THE EXACT SAME PRICE!

FUN FOR THE KIDDIES
Reindeer Jerky!
Krusty
REINDEER
Jerky
NEW
TAKE THESE COMICS AN' STUFF 'EM...IN YOUR STOCKINGS!
BUT PLEASE, NOT IN YOUR PANTS
(YOU HOOLIGANS KNOW WHO YOU ARE!)
COMICS
COMICS
KIDS!
Fly like a reindeer
(and bounce off the walls)
with
BUZZ
Cola!
BUZZ
FOR THE GROWN-UPS
NAUGHTY MAGAZINES WITH NAKED LADIES!
Girlie
Nothing at all to do with Christmas, but we've got them!
Photos with Santa - $20!
Thank You
COME AGAIN!

Christmas Eve on
Mammon
Street

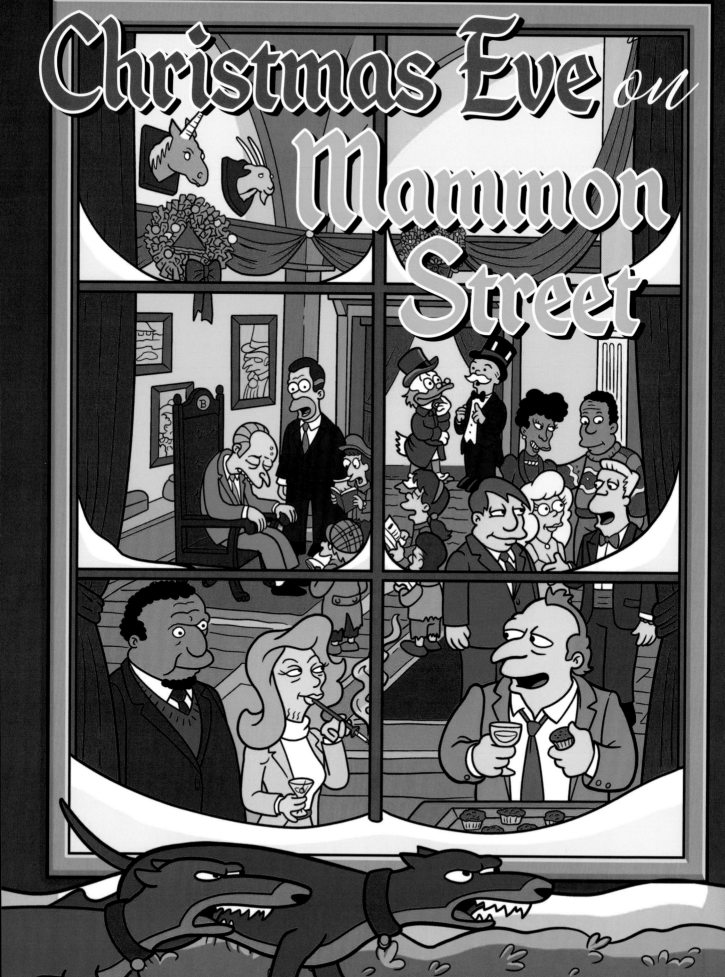

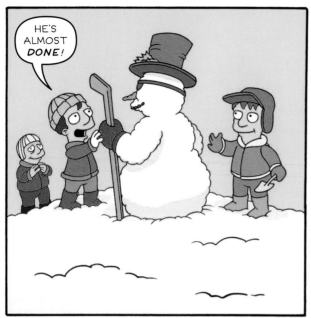

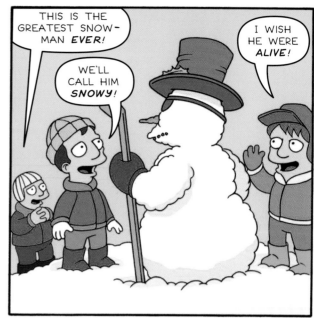

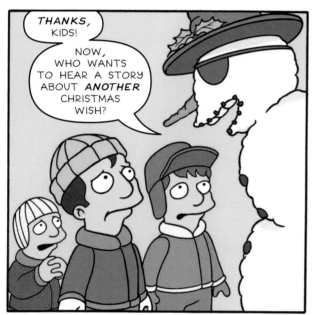

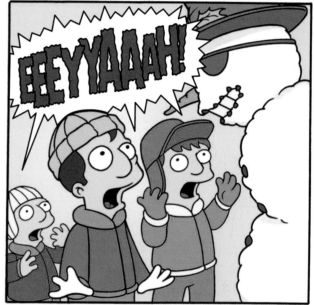

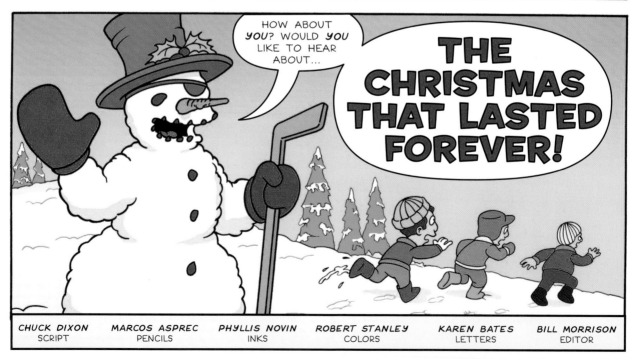

CHUCK DIXON
SCRIPT

MARCOS ASPREC
PENCILS

PHYLLIS NOVIN
INKS

ROBERT STANLEY
COLORS

KAREN BATES
LETTERS

BILL MORRISON
EDITOR

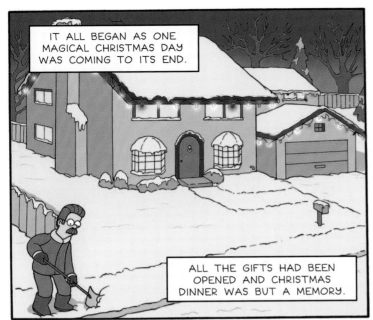

IT ALL BEGAN AS ONE MAGICAL CHRISTMAS DAY WAS COMING TO ITS END.

ALL THE GIFTS HAD BEEN OPENED AND CHRISTMAS DINNER WAS BUT A MEMORY.

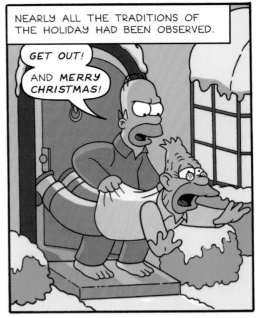

NEARLY ALL THE TRADITIONS OF THE HOLIDAY HAD BEEN OBSERVED.

GET OUT!

AND *MERRY CHRISTMAS!*

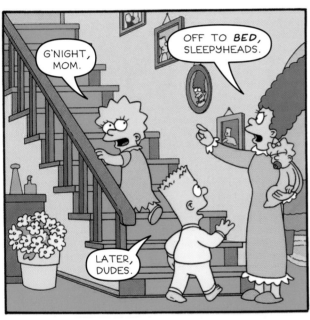

G'NIGHT, MOM.

OFF TO *BED,* SLEEPYHEADS.

LATER, DUDES.

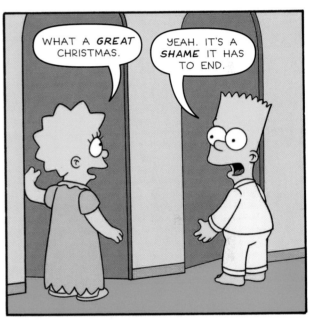

WHAT A *GREAT* CHRISTMAS.

YEAH. IT'S A *SHAME* IT HAS TO END.

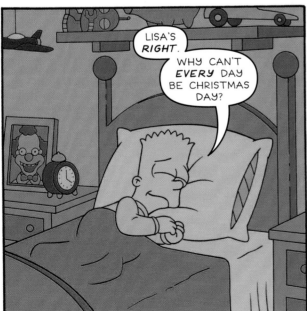

LISA'S *RIGHT.* WHY CAN'T *EVERY* DAY BE CHRISTMAS DAY?

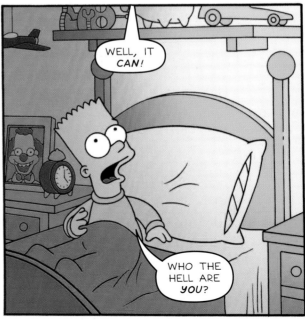

WELL, IT *CAN!*

WHO THE HELL ARE *YOU?*

I'M A CHRISTMAS ANGEL, BART.
WOW. I'VE NEVER SEEN A CHRISTMAS FAIRY!
ANGEL, BART. CHRISTMAS ANGEL. I'M HERE TO GRANT CHILDREN'S WISHES.
LIKE IN "THE NIGHT THEY ARRESTED SANTA"?
NO...
"THE CITY THAT BANNED CHRISTMAS"?
NO...
"THE ATHEIST ON 34TH STREET"?
NO!
NONE OF THEM!
I'M HERE FOR YOU, BART. TO MAKE YOUR FONDEST CHRISTMAS WISH COME TRUE.
A CHAINSAW?
THE ONE YOU MADE ABOUT EVERY DAY BEING CHRISTMAS.
REALLY?
OBOYOBOY OBOYOBOYOBOY OBOY!

NOW TUCK YOURSELF IN AND DREAM DREAMS OF YULETIDE SPLENDOR.
WHEN YOU AWAKEN, EVERY DAY WILL BE CHRISTMAS DAY...FOREVER!
MERRY CHRISTMAS, FAIRY.
ANGEL!
THE VERY NEXT MORNING...
WHAT A FREAKY DREAM!
I HAD THE WEIRDEST DREAM, LIS. I DREAMT IT WAS CHRISTMAS ALL OVER AGAIN TODAY.
BUT IT IS CHRISTMAS TODAY, BART.
WHAT?
IT'S CHRISTMAS.
NO SCHOOL?
YES.
PRESENTS?
YES!
I DON'T SEE WHAT THE BIG DEAL IS.
WOO-HOO!

HUH?
THAT FAIRY'S A PHONY!
WHO WANTS TURKEY OMELETS?
AN ANGEL TOLD ME THAT HE'D GRANT MY WISH AND MAKE EVERY DAY CHRISTMAS!
BUT EVERY DAY IS CHRISTMAS, BART.
BUT THIS IS ALL WRONG!
IT'S THE SAME CHRISTMAS ALL OVER AGAIN, NOT A NEW CHRISTMAS.
AND I'VE ALTERED REALITY FOREVER.
OH WELL.
AT LEAST I DON'T HAVE SCHOOL.
EVERYONE GET DRESSED FOR CHURCH.
D'OH!

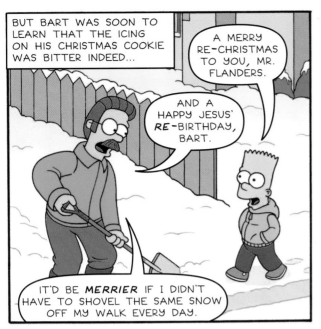

BUT BART WAS SOON TO LEARN THAT THE ICING ON HIS CHRISTMAS COOKIE WAS BITTER INDEED...

A MERRY RE-CHRISTMAS TO YOU, MR. FLANDERS.

AND A HAPPY JESUS' *RE*-BIRTHDAY, BART.

IT'D BE *MERRIER* IF I DIDN'T HAVE TO SHOVEL THE SAME SNOW OFF MY WALK EVERY DAY.

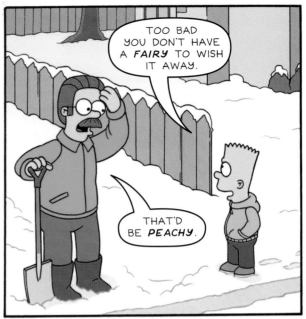

TOO BAD YOU DON'T HAVE A *FAIRY* TO WISH IT AWAY.

THAT'D BE *PEACHY*.

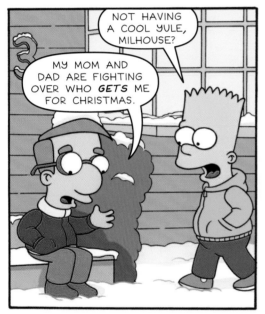

NOT HAVING A COOL YULE, MILHOUSE?

MY MOM AND DAD ARE FIGHTING OVER WHO *GETS* ME FOR CHRISTMAS.

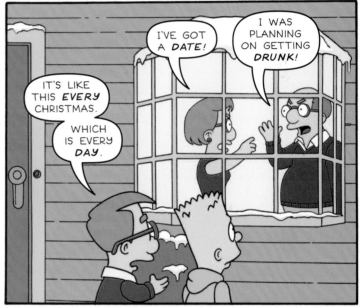

I'VE GOT A *DATE*!

I WAS PLANNING ON GETTING *DRUNK*!

IT'S LIKE THIS *EVERY* CHRISTMAS.

WHICH IS EVERY *DAY*.

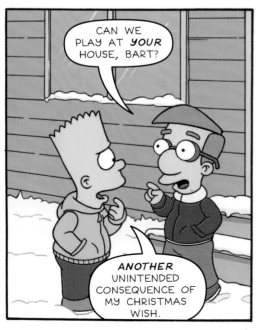

CAN WE PLAY AT *YOUR* HOUSE, BART?

ANOTHER UNINTENDED CONSEQUENCE OF MY CHRISTMAS WISH.

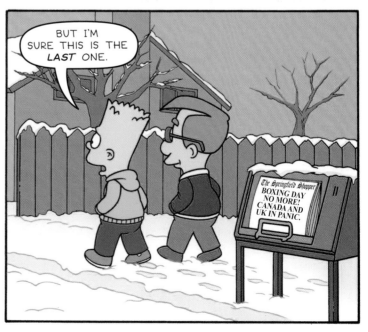

BUT I'M SURE THIS IS THE *LAST* ONE.

The Springfield Shopper
BOXING DAY NO MORE! CANADA AND UK IN PANIC.

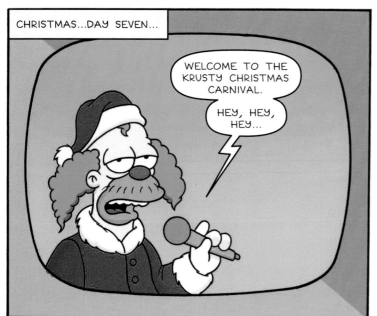

CHRISTMAS...DAY SEVEN...

WELCOME TO THE KRUSTY CHRISTMAS CARNIVAL.

HEY, HEY, HEY...

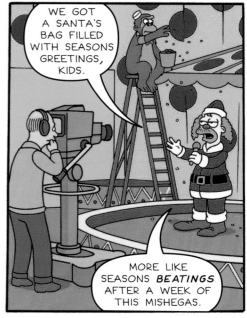

WE GOT A SANTA'S BAG FILLED WITH SEASONS GREETINGS, KIDS.

MORE LIKE SEASONS *BEATINGS* AFTER A WEEK OF THIS MISHEGAS.

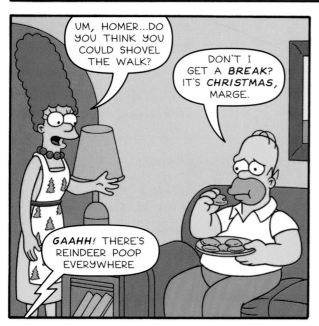

UM, HOMER...DO YOU THINK YOU COULD SHOVEL THE WALK?

DON'T I GET A *BREAK*? IT'S *CHRISTMAS*, MARGE.

GAAHH! THERE'S REINDEER POOP EVERYWHERE

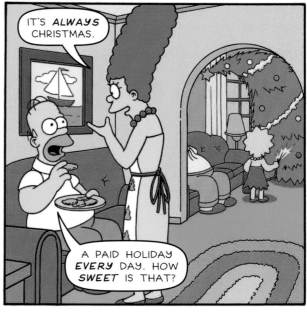

IT'S *ALWAYS* CHRISTMAS.

A PAID HOLIDAY *EVERY* DAY. HOW *SWEET* IS THAT?

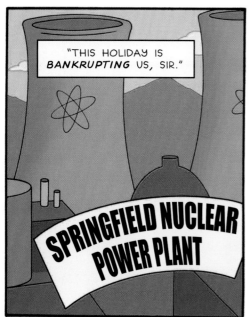

"THIS HOLIDAY IS *BANKRUPTING* US, SIR."

SPRINGFIELD NUCLEAR POWER PLANT

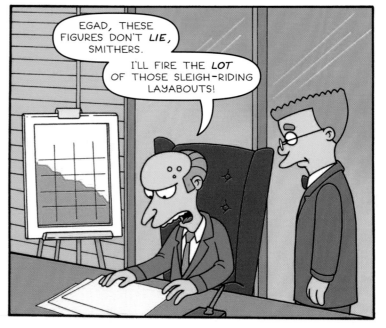

EGAD, THESE FIGURES DON'T *LIE*, SMITHERS.

I'LL FIRE THE *LOT* OF THOSE SLEIGH-RIDING LAYABOUTS!

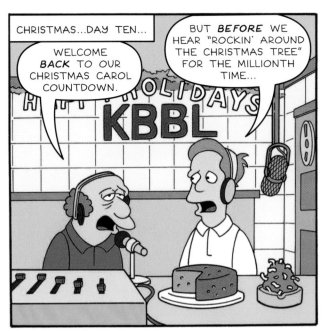

CHRISTMAS...DAY TEN...

WELCOME *BACK* TO OUR CHRISTMAS CAROL COUNTDOWN.

BUT *BEFORE* WE HEAR "ROCKIN' AROUND THE CHRISTMAS TREE" FOR THE MILLIONTH TIME...

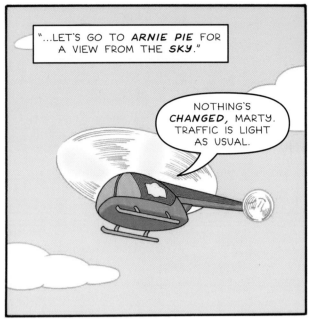

"...LET'S GO TO *ARNIE PIE* FOR A VIEW FROM THE *SKY*."

NOTHING'S *CHANGED*, MARTY. TRAFFIC IS LIGHT AS USUAL.

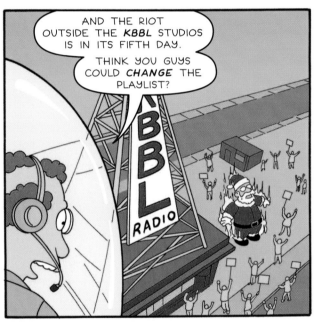

AND THE RIOT OUTSIDE THE *KBBL* STUDIOS IS IN ITS FIFTH DAY.

THINK YOU GUYS COULD *CHANGE* THE PLAYLIST?

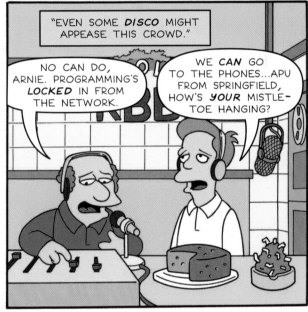

"EVEN SOME *DISCO* MIGHT APPEASE THIS CROWD."

NO CAN DO, ARNIE. PROGRAMMING'S *LOCKED* IN FROM THE NETWORK.

WE *CAN* GO TO THE PHONES...APU FROM SPRINGFIELD, HOW'S *YOUR* MISTLE-TOE HANGING?

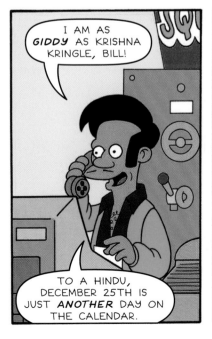

I AM AS *GIDDY* AS KRISHNA KRINGLE, BILL!

TO A HINDU, DECEMBER 25TH IS JUST *ANOTHER* DAY ON THE CALENDAR.

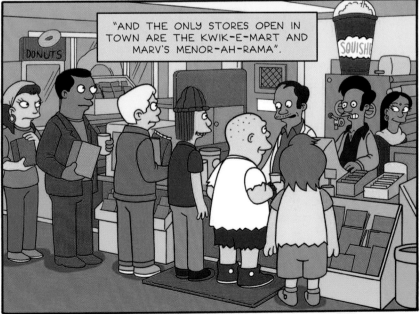

"AND THE ONLY STORES OPEN IN TOWN ARE THE KWIK-E-MART AND MARV'S MENOR-AH-RAMA".

CHRISTMAS...DAY ELEVEN...
MERRY--
DING!
DING!
SAY IT AND YOU'RE A **DEAD** SANTA, SANTA.
CHRISTMAS...DAY THIRTEEN...
...AND **STILL** NO BONUS CHECK FOR GIL!
CHRISTMAS...DAY SIXTEEN...
WHEN ARE YOU GOING BACK TO WORK, SEYMOUR?
APPARENTLY **NEVER,** MOTHER.
CHRISTMAS...DAY EIGHTEEN...
CHRISTMAS...DAY TWENTY...
BLEH. NO BEER AND NOW **THIS**.
WHAT ARE WE DRINKING, MOE?
COUGH SYRUP.

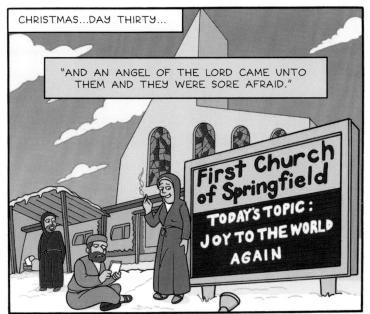

CHRISTMAS...DAY THIRTY...

"AND AN ANGEL OF THE LORD CAME UNTO THEM AND THEY WERE SORE AFRAID."

First Church of Springfield

TODAY'S TOPIC: JOY TO THE WORLD AGAIN

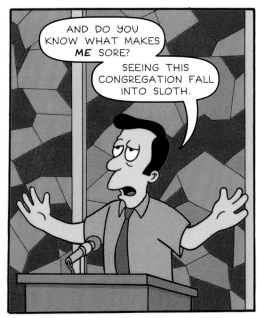

AND DO YOU KNOW WHAT MAKES *ME* SORE?

SEEING THIS CONGREGATION FALL INTO SLOTH.

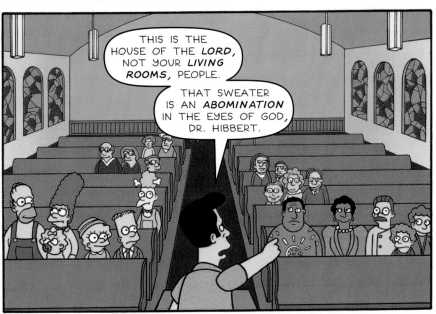

THIS IS THE HOUSE OF THE *LORD*, NOT YOUR *LIVING ROOMS*, PEOPLE.

THAT SWEATER IS AN *ABOMINATION* IN THE EYES OF GOD, DR. HIBBERT.

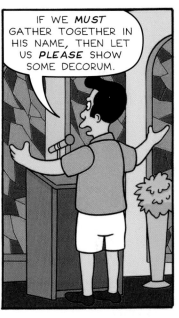

IF WE *MUST* GATHER TOGETHER IN HIS NAME, THEN LET US *PLEASE* SHOW SOME DECORUM.

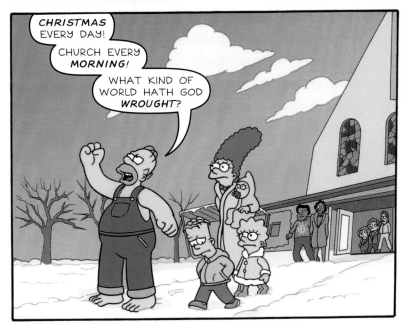

CHRISTMAS EVERY DAY!

CHURCH EVERY *MORNING*!

WHAT KIND OF WORLD HATH GOD *WROUGHT*?

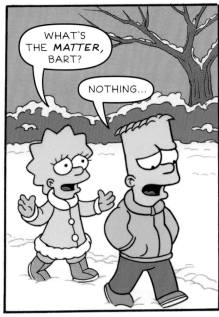

WHAT'S THE *MATTER*, BART?

NOTHING...

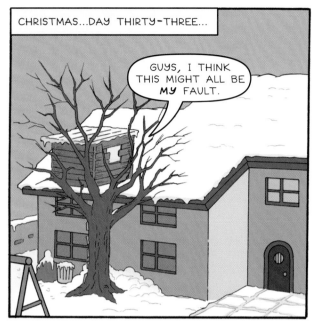

CHRISTMAS...DAY THIRTY-THREE...

GUYS, I THINK THIS MIGHT ALL BE *MY* FAULT.

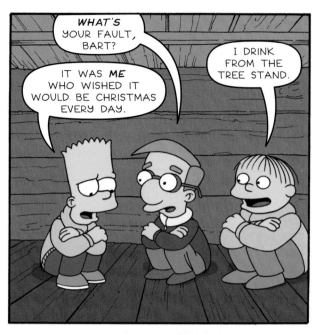

WHAT'S YOUR FAULT, BART?

IT WAS *ME* WHO WISHED IT WOULD BE CHRISTMAS EVERY DAY.

I DRINK FROM THE TREE STAND.

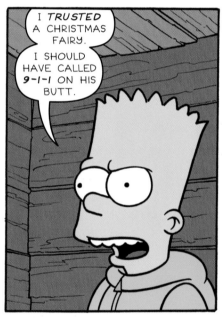

I *TRUSTED* A CHRISTMAS FAIRY. I SHOULD HAVE CALLED *9-1-1* ON HIS BUTT.

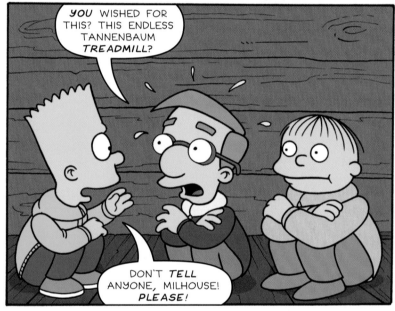

YOU WISHED FOR THIS? THIS ENDLESS TANNENBAUM *TREADMILL*?

DON'T *TELL* ANYONE, MILHOUSE! *PLEASE!*

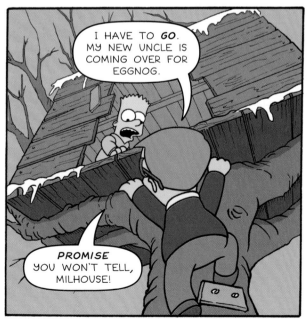

I HAVE TO *GO*. MY NEW UNCLE IS COMING OVER FOR EGGNOG.

PROMISE YOU WON'T TELL, MILHOUSE!

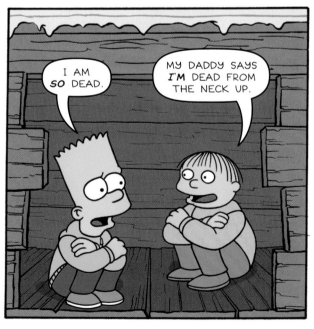

I AM *SO* DEAD.

MY DADDY SAYS *I'M* DEAD FROM THE NECK UP.

THE TIME IT TAKES TO FORM AN ANGRY MOB LATER...
BART! BART! BART!
NO PAY-CHECKS!
NO MAIL!
NO CIGARETTES OR BOOZE!
THIS IS WORSE THAN USUAL.
IT'S PROBABLY THE BIGGEST, ANGRIEST MOB I'VE SEEN SINCE--
CRASH!
OH!
THEY WANT TO KILL OUR LITTLE BOY!
AND THE FRUITCAKE IS STALE.
IT'S TIME TO FACE THE CAROLERS, PEOPLE.
BART!
NO!

I'M THE ONE YOU WANT!
DON'T TAKE YOUR ANGER OUT ON MY FAMILY!
WHY, IT'S JUST A CHILD!
SO'S ALL WE GOTTA DO IS AIM LOWER.
END XMAS NOW!!
NO! LET'S LISTEN TO WHAT HE HAS TO SAY!
ALL I WANTED WAS FOR THE JOY OF THE SEASON TO LAST MORE THAN ONE DAY.
I DIDN'T KNOW MY WISH WOULD GO ALL TWILIGHT ZONE ON ME.
BART SPEAKS THE TRUTH.
HIS WISH WAS THE SIMPLE DESIRE OF AN INNOCENT CHILD.
THAT'S HIM! THAT'S THE FREAK WHO STARTED ALL THIS!

WOW, A CHRISTMAS FAIRY!
I'M AN ANGEL. AND I'M MARRIED, OKAY?
LOOK INTO YOUR HEARTS, PEOPLE OF SPRINGFIELD.
HAVE THE PAST FEW WEEKS BEEN SO TERRIBLE? AND IF THEY HAVE IT'S BECAUSE YOU HAVE NOT EMBRACED THE YULE SPIRIT.
JUST IMAGINE A WORLD WITHOUT CHRISTMAS.
HMMM...
LAS VEGAS...
AND NOW THAT YOU'VE ALL LEARNED YOUR LESSON...
...I'LL REVERSE THE WISH AND TOMORROW WILL BE DECEMBER 26TH!
UNNH!
NOT SO FAST, WINGS.

THAT'S RIGHT! IT'S THE SNOWMAN WHO'S BEEN NARRATING THIS STORY!
AND I WANT IT TO STAY CHRISTMAS FOREVER SO I'LL NEVER MELT!
SO YOU CAN CONTINUE DELIGHTING CHILDREN ALL THE YEAR 'ROUND?
NO! BECAUSE MELTING SUCKS!
IT'S GOING TO STAY WINTER AND THERE'S NOTHING YOU CAN DO ABOUT IT!
UM... CAREFUL WITH THOSE TORCHES AND SNOW SHOVELS, ALL RIGHT?
THE NEXT MORNING...
FINALLY, THE DAY AFTER CHRISTMAS.
WELL, HOMER, THINGS ARE BACK TO THE WAY THEY SHOULD BE.
BUT THE CHRISTMAS SPIRIT LIVES ON IN ALL OF US, BOY.
GOD BLESS US EVERY ONE.
AND THAT'S THE END!
EXALL
Gasoline
Duff

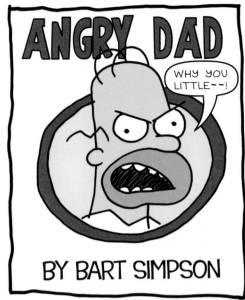

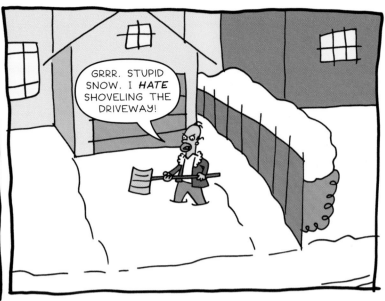

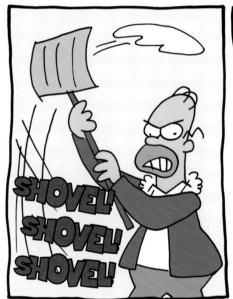

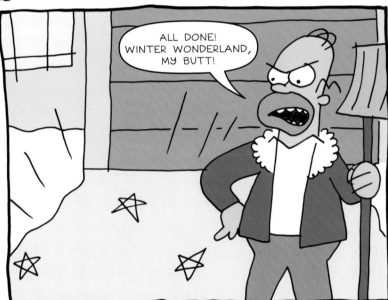

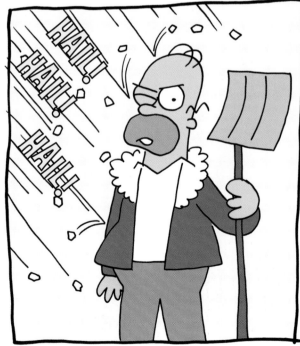

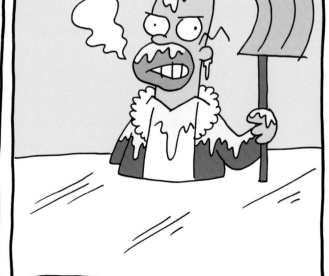

TONY DIGEROLAMO
SCRIPT

JASON HO
PENCILS & INKS

CHRIS UNGAR
COLORS

KAREN BATES
LETTERS

BILL MORRISON
EDITOR

GAAAAAAH!
PICK!
HACK!
HACK!
PICK!
GWAAAAAAAH!
WACKA-WACKA! WACKA-WACKA!
FWAAAAAAAAH!
FWOOOOSH!
FWOOOOSH!
ALMOST DONE. GRRR. JUST NEED TO THAW MY FEET--
CRACKLE CRACKLE
UH-OH!
KRACK!
YIPE!

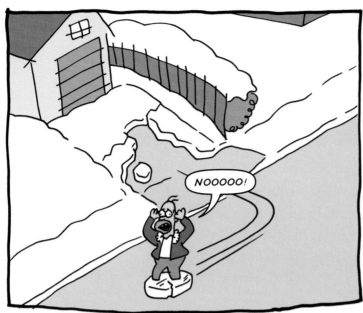

NOOOOO!

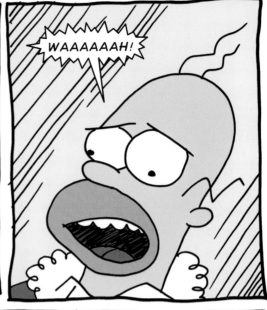

WAAAAAAH!

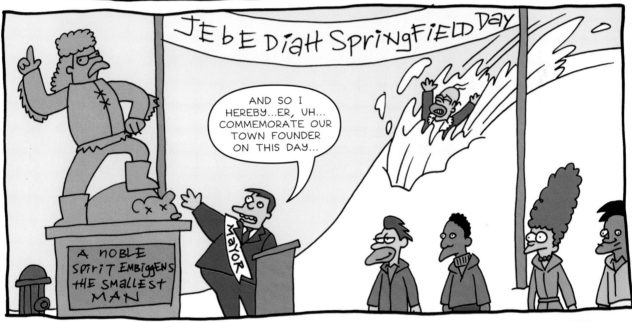

JEBEDIAH SpringFIELD Day

AND SO I HEREBY...ER, UH... COMMEMORATE OUR TOWN FOUNDER ON THIS DAY...

A NOBLE SPIRIT EMBIGGENS THE SMALLEST MAN

MAYOR

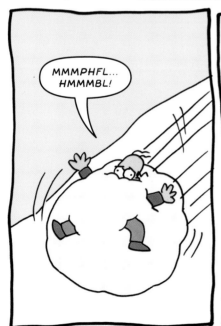

MMMPHFL... HMMMBL!

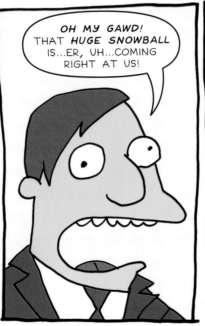

OH MY GAWD! THAT HUGE SNOWBALL IS...ER, UH...COMING RIGHT AT US!

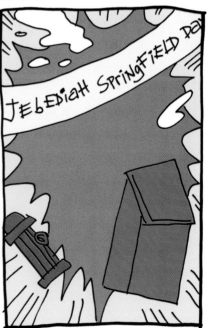

JEBEDIAH SpringFIELD Day

JEBEDIAH SPRINGF
A NOBLE SPIRIT EMBIGGENS THE SMALLEST MAN
LIKE THE STATUE SAYS, "A SNOWBALL SPIRIT EMBIGGENS THE SMALLEST STRIP!"
BWA-HA-HA!
WHUH-OH!
WHY YOU LITTLE--! I'LL EMBIGGEN YOU!
ACK!
THE END

ITCHY & SCRATCHY in
THE GIFT THAT KEEPS ON GIVING
HAPPY HANUKKAH, SCRATCHY!
OOH, THANK YOU!
TICK TICK TICK
BOOM SHKY
EEEERGH GEVALT!
HA HA!
WATER! WATER!
HA HA HA!
SPLASHY
AAAAH!
PFHPHHHHH
YEEAARGHH!
HEE HEE HEEEE!
LONG-LASTING MIRACLE OIL
8 Days Later
IT STILL BURNS...
WEE-HEEEE!
LONG-LASTING MIRACLE OIL

HAPPY HANUKKAH
WOW, HEY! PRETTY HOT, EH, KIDS?
THE LAST TIME MY TUCHUS BURNED FOR EIGHT DAYS WAS AFTER I ATE A HEAT LAMP DOG FROM THE KWIK-E-MART! OY! LET ME TELL YOU!
NEED A YARMULKE, TAKE A YARMULKE. HAVE A YARMULKE? SUCH A NICE BOY.
ANYWAY, WELCOME BACK TO THE ALL-SINGING, ALL-DANCING, ALL SHVITZING KRUSTY HANUKKAH SPECIAL!
WOO-HOO-HA HA!
SHPRITZ!
GBBGBKL!
NOW, KIDS...IF I MAY TAKE A MOMENT HERE TO GET SERIOUS, SEE, I GOT A LITTLE STORY TO TELL YOU.
IT'S ABOUT THE WORST HANUKKAH A CLOWN EVER HAD. AND THAT CLOWN WAS ME, KIDS. YEP, YOUR OL' PAL KRUSTY.
I CALL THIS STORY "THE GIFT OF THE MACCABEES!"
I, UH, SAID IT OUT LOUD IN CASE ANY OF YOU DUMB KIDS CAN'T READ.
THE GIFT OF THE MACCABEE

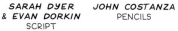

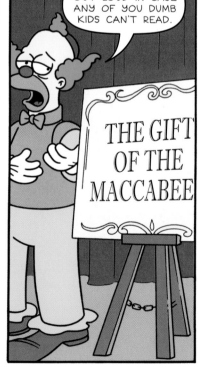

SARAH DYER & EVAN DORKIN SCRIPT | **JOHN COSTANZA** PENCILS | **PHYLLIS NOVIN** INKS | **ART VILLANUEVA** COLORS | **KAREN BATES** LETTERS | **BILL MORRISON** EDITOR

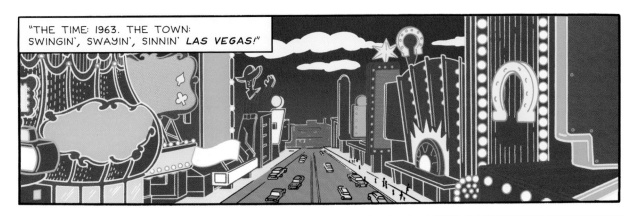

"THE TIME: 1963. THE TOWN: SWINGIN', SWAYIN', SINNIN' *LAS VEGAS!*"

"THE CLOWN: KRUSTY. BACK THEN I WAS WORKING THE MAIN LOUNGE AT MOISHE'S KOSHER CASINO AND DELI, FIVE SHOWS A NIGHT, EVERY NIGHT EXCEPT FRIDAY."

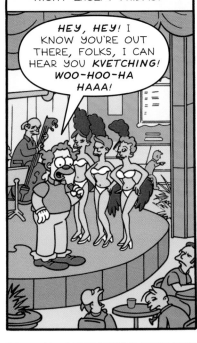

HEY, *HEY!* I KNOW YOU'RE OUT THERE, FOLKS, I CAN HEAR YOU *KVETCHING!* WOO-HOO-HA HAAA!

"AND THE GIRL. SHE WAS MORE THAN JUST A GIRL, SHE WAS A *SHOWGIRL!* AND WHAT A SHOW, OOH-WOW-WOW-A-WOWEE!"

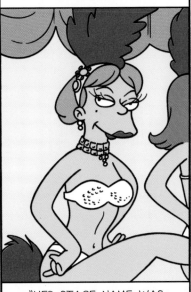

"HER STAGE NAME WAS *JEWEL STARR.* BUT I FOUND OUT HER REAL NAME. *GLENNA MESHUGAWITZ.*"

"SHE WAS PRETTY, AND NICE. BUT BEST OF ALL..."

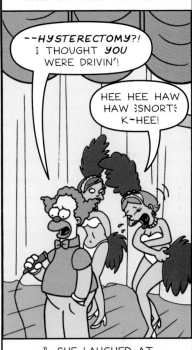

--*HYSTERECTOMY?!* I THOUGHT *YOU* WERE DRIVIN'!

HEE HEE HAW HAW ⸢SNORT⸣ K-HEE!

"...SHE LAUGHED AT ALL OF MY JOKES."

"WE'D BEEN DATING FOR A WHILE, AND WITH HANUKKAH COMIN' UP I WANTED TO IMPRESS HER WITH GIFTS SO GOOD SHE'D PLOTZ."

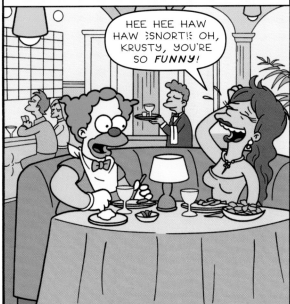

HEE HEE HAW HAW ⸢SNORT!⸣ OH, KRUSTY, YOU'RE SO *FUNNY!*

"UNFORTUNATELY, I FOUND MYSELF LOW ON CASH AFTER A SERIES OF BAD INVESTMENTS."

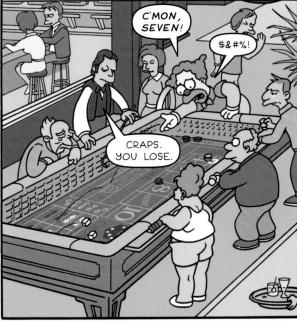

C'MON, SEVEN!

$&#%!

CRAPS. YOU LOSE.

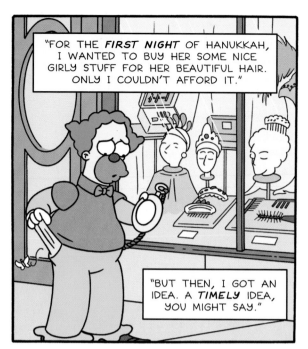

"FOR THE *FIRST NIGHT* OF HANUKKAH, I WANTED TO BUY HER SOME NICE GIRLY STUFF FOR HER BEAUTIFUL HAIR. ONLY I COULDN'T AFFORD IT."

"BUT THEN, I GOT AN IDEA. A *TIMELY* IDEA, YOU MIGHT SAY."

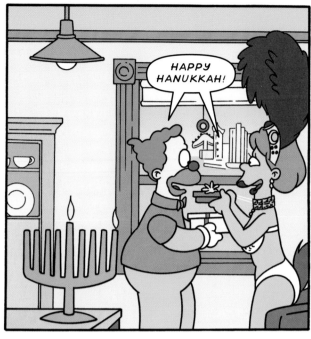

HAPPY HANUKKAH!

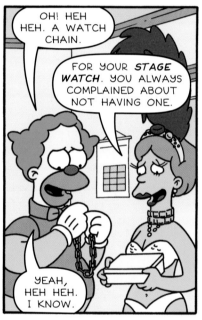

OH! HEH HEH. A WATCH CHAIN.

FOR YOUR *STAGE WATCH.* YOU ALWAYS COMPLAINED ABOUT NOT HAVING ONE.

YEAH, HEH HEH. I KNOW.

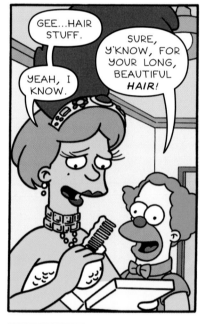

GEE...HAIR STUFF.

SURE, Y'KNOW, FOR YOUR LONG, BEAUTIFUL *HAIR!*

YEAH, I KNOW.

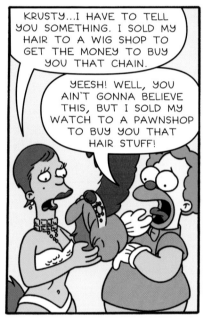

KRUSTY...I HAVE TO TELL YOU SOMETHING. I SOLD MY HAIR TO A WIG SHOP TO GET THE MONEY TO BUY YOU THAT CHAIN.

YEESH! WELL, YOU AIN'T GONNA BELIEVE THIS, BUT I SOLD MY WATCH TO A PAWNSHOP TO BUY YOU THAT HAIR STUFF!

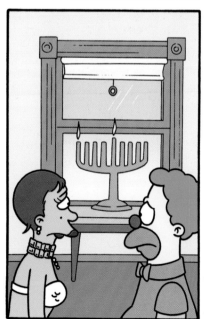

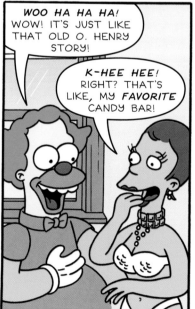

WOO HA HA HA! WOW! IT'S JUST LIKE THAT OLD O. HENRY STORY!

K-HEE HEE! RIGHT? THAT'S LIKE, MY *FAVORITE* CANDY BAR!

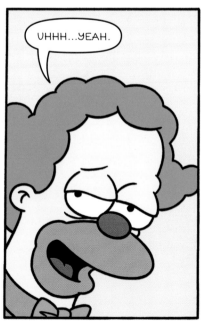

UHHH...YEAH.

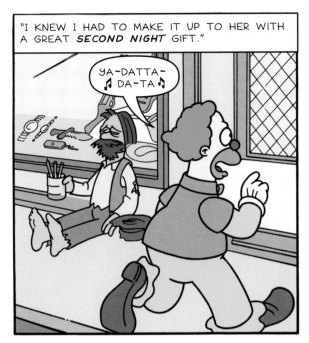

"I KNEW I HAD TO MAKE IT UP TO HER WITH A GREAT *SECOND NIGHT* GIFT."

YA-DATTA-♪DA-TA♪

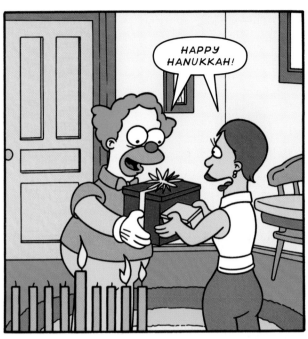

HAPPY HANUKKAH!

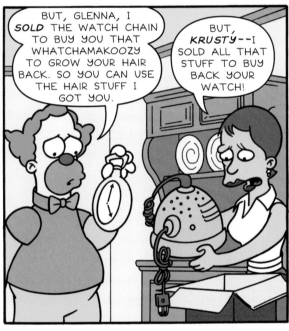

BUT, GLENNA, I *SOLD* THE WATCH CHAIN TO BUY YOU THAT WHATCHAMAKOOZY TO GROW YOUR HAIR BACK. SO YOU CAN USE THE HAIR STUFF I GOT YOU.

BUT, *KRUSTY*--I SOLD ALL THAT STUFF TO BUY BACK YOUR WATCH!

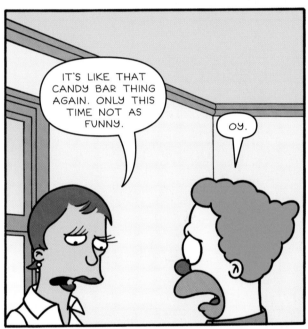

IT'S LIKE THAT CANDY BAR THING AGAIN. ONLY THIS TIME NOT AS FUNNY.

OY.

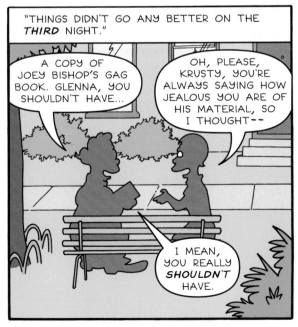

"THINGS DIDN'T GO ANY BETTER ON THE *THIRD* NIGHT."

A COPY OF JOEY BISHOP'S GAG BOOK. GLENNA, YOU SHOULDN'T HAVE...

OH, PLEASE, KRUSTY, YOU'RE ALWAYS SAYING HOW JEALOUS YOU ARE OF HIS MATERIAL, SO I THOUGHT--

I MEAN, YOU REALLY *SHOULDN'T* HAVE.

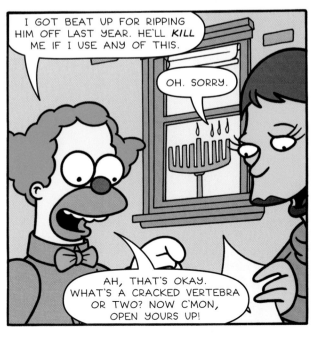

I GOT BEAT UP FOR RIPPING HIM OFF LAST YEAR. HE'LL *KILL* ME IF I USE ANY OF THIS.

OH. SORRY.

AH, THAT'S OKAY. WHAT'S A CRACKED VERTEBRA OR TWO? NOW C'MON, OPEN YOURS UP!

OH, KRUSTY, IT'S LOVELY!
LIKE IT? REAL GENUINE SOMETHIN' OR OTHER! I GOT IT FROM A GUY WHO SAID IT FELL OFF A TRUCK. AFTER, Y'KNOW, A LITTLE NUDGE.
OH, KRUSTY, IT'S B-BEAUTIFUL. SNIFF
HUH? KRUSTY, WHAT'S HAPPENING TO MY NECKLACE?! IT'S MELTING FROM MY TEARS!
OY, ROCK CANDY! I BEEN SWINDLED!
"THE FOURTH NIGHT WAS YET ANOTHER STINKEROO."
OOOCHY. SEE, I KINDA MISSED SOME PAYMENTS ON MY HI-FI AND THEY, UH, KINDA REPOSSESSED IT. AHEH.
THE CONDESCENDING STEVE ALLEN AND MY SON, THE PINKO
Jose Jiminez sings TOSCANINI
BUT SO WHAT, RIGHT? JUST WAIT'LL YOU SEE WHAT I GOT YA!
SHPLOOSH
OOH, DOUBLE OOCHY. SEE, THAT WAS A BEAUTIFUL LIFE-SIZE ICE SCULPTURE OF YOUR HEAD. HONEST, GOOD ENOUGH TO NECK WITH!
I GUESS I SHOULD'VE PUT THAT BABY IN THE FREEZER. HEH HEH.
"NIGHT FIVE? THE LESS SAID, THE BETTER."
I HATE FUDGE.

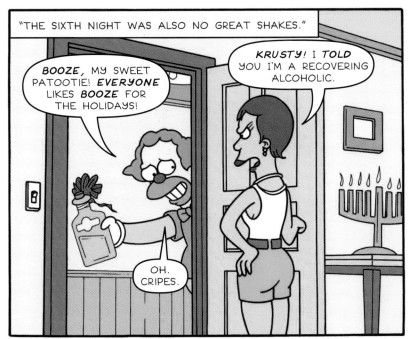

"THE SIXTH NIGHT WAS ALSO NO GREAT SHAKES."

BOOZE, MY SWEET PATOOTIE! EVERYONE LIKES BOOZE FOR THE HOLIDAYS!

KRUSTY! I TOLD YOU I'M A RECOVERING ALCOHOLIC.

OH. CRIPES.

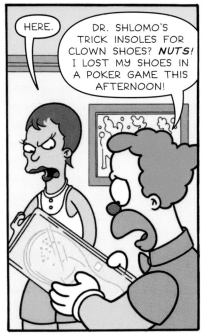

HERE.

DR. SHLOMO'S TRICK INSOLES FOR CLOWN SHOES? NUTS! I LOST MY SHOES IN A POKER GAME THIS AFTERNOON!

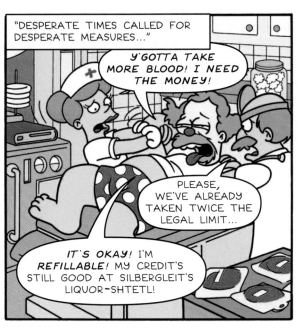

"DESPERATE TIMES CALLED FOR DESPERATE MEASURES..."

Y'GOTTA TAKE MORE BLOOD! I NEED THE MONEY!

PLEASE, WE'VE ALREADY TAKEN TWICE THE LEGAL LIMIT...

IT'S OKAY! I'M REFILLABLE! MY CREDIT'S STILL GOOD AT SILBERGLEIT'S LIQUOR-SHTETL!

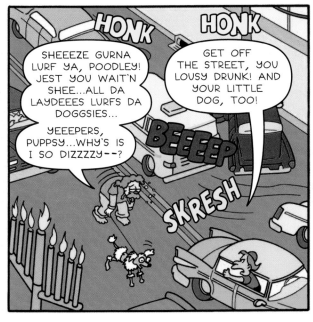

HONK   HONK

SHEEEZE GURNA LURF YA, POODLEY! JEST YOU WAIT'N SHEE...ALL DA LAYDEEES LURFS DA DOGGSIES...

YEEEPERS, PUPPSY...WHY'S IS I SO DIZZZZY--?

GET OFF THE STREET, YOU LOUSY DRUNK! AND YOUR LITTLE DOG, TOO!

BEEEEP

SKRESH

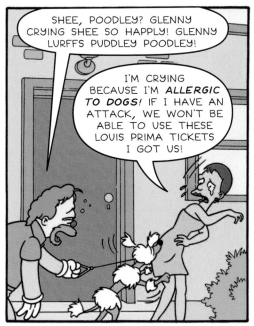

SHEE, POODLEY? GLENNY CRYING SHEE SO HAPPLY! GLENNY LURFFS PUDDLEY POODLEY!

I'M CRYING BECAUSE I'M ALLERGIC TO DOGS! IF I HAVE AN ATTACK, WE WON'T BE ABLE TO USE THESE LOUIS PRIMA TICKETS I GOT US!

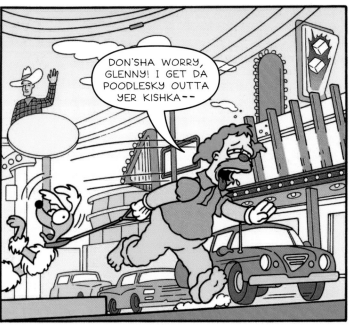

DON'SHA WORRY, GLENNY! I GET DA POODLESKY OUTTA YER KISHKA--

ERRRRRT
B-KRUSTNCH!
AAAAGH!
WOOF WOOF
THIS CLOWN NEEDS BLOOD! LOTS OF BLOOD!
ANYBODY NEED TWO TICKETS TO SEE PRIMA TONIGHT?
OYYYYY, VEZ MEAR...
"FINALLY, WITH ONLY ONE CHANCE LEFT, I FOUND MYSELF AT HER DOOR. I HAD NOTHING LEFT TO GIVE HER..."
"...EXCEPT MY HEART."
I.O.U. 8 BETTER GIFTS. LOVE, KRUSTY
"I SLIPPED THE NOTE UNDER HER DOOR AND WAITED. TWO MINUTES LATER, I GOT MY REPLY."
OH BOY-HOY-HOY!
KRUSTY, I GIVE YOU YOUR FREEDOM. HAPPY HANUKKAH, YOU CREEP. -G. P.S. STAY AWAY FROM ME OR ELSE. I KNOW PEOPLE.
"I NEVER SAW HER AGAIN. SHE FOUND WORK AS A DANCER IN JOEY BISHOP'S SHOW."
WAAAAAAAAHHH!!!
"I COULDN'T EVEN AFFORD A TICKET TO SEE HER AGAIN."

AND THERE YOU HAVE IT. MY WORST HANUKKAH EVER.
OH, MAN, THAT WAS GREAT!
HA! HA!
HA!
HA!
HA!
HA! HA!
OY OY OY! I'M DYING HERE! WHAT A YUTZ MY SON IS!
HEY. HEY! WHAT ARE YOU LOUSY KIDS LAUGHIN' AT?
IT'S NOT FUNNY! STOP LAUGHING! STOP--
NEED A YARMULKE, TAKE A YARMULKE. HAVE A YARMULKE? SUCH A NICE BOY.
I GUESS IT WAS KIND OF FUNNY... ...I MEAN, WHAT A CRAPPY HANUKKAH, HUH, KIDS? I WOULDN'T WISH THAT ON MY AGENT! BAH-BOOMSKY!
WOO-HOO-HA HA!
HA HA HA! AHHHH-HA HAAA HAAAA HAAAAA--!
AW GEEZ, I CAN'T TAKE SEVEN MORE NIGHTS OF THIS!
WAAAAH HAA-HAAAA-HAAAAAA--!
THE END

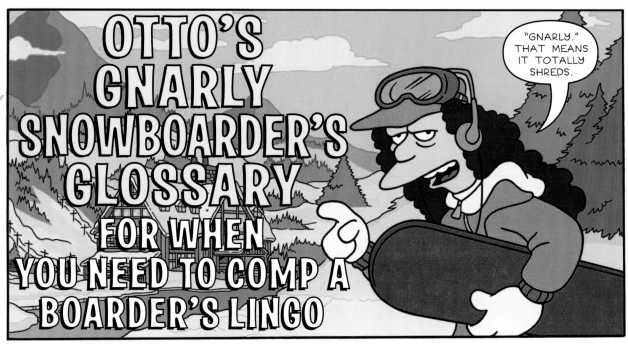

OTTO'S GNARLY SNOWBOARDER'S GLOSSARY

FOR WHEN YOU NEED TO COMP A BOARDER'S LINGO

"GNARLY." THAT MEANS IT TOTALLY SHREDS.

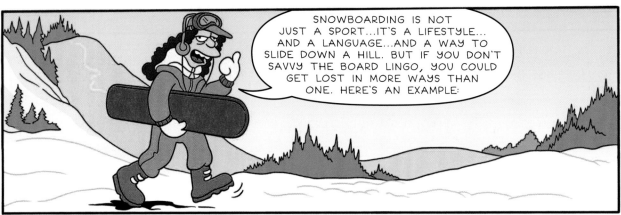

SNOWBOARDING IS NOT JUST A SPORT...IT'S A LIFESTYLE... AND A LANGUAGE...AND A WAY TO SLIDE DOWN A HILL. BUT IF YOU DON'T SAVVY THE BOARD LINGO, YOU COULD GET LOST IN MORE WAYS THAN ONE. HERE'S AN EXAMPLE:

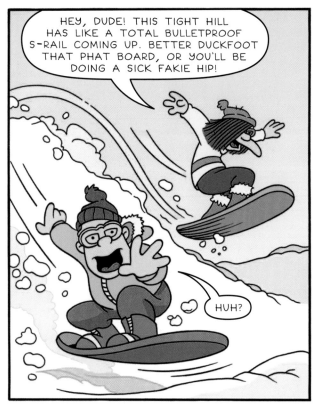

HEY, DUDE! THIS TIGHT HILL HAS LIKE A TOTAL BULLETPROOF S-RAIL COMING UP. BETTER DUCKFOOT THAT PHAT BOARD, OR YOU'LL BE DOING A SICK FAKIE HIP!

HUH?

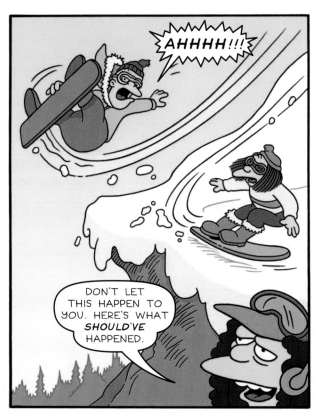

AHHHH!!!

DON'T LET THIS HAPPEN TO YOU. HERE'S WHAT *SHOULD'VE* HAPPENED.

TONY DIGEROLAMO
SCRIPT

CARLOS VALENTI
PENCILS

STEVE STEERE, JR.
INKS

ROBERT STANLEY
COLORS

KAREN BATES
LETTERS

BILL MORRISON
EDITOR

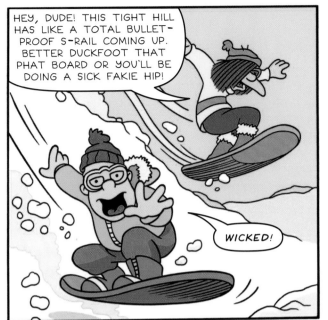

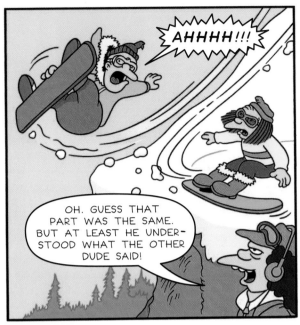

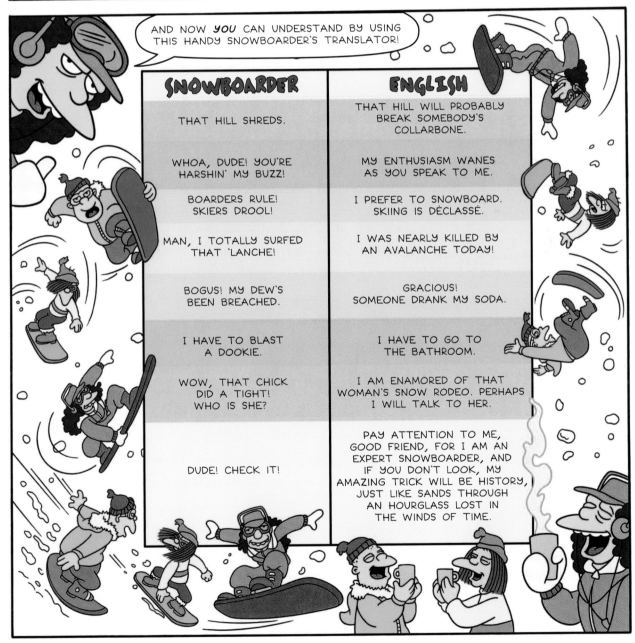

SNOWBOARDER	ENGLISH
THAT HILL SHREDS.	THAT HILL WILL PROBABLY BREAK SOMEBODY'S COLLARBONE.
WHOA, DUDE! YOU'RE HARSHIN' MY BUZZ!	MY ENTHUSIASM WANES AS YOU SPEAK TO ME.
BOARDERS RULE! SKIERS DROOL!	I PREFER TO SNOWBOARD. SKIING IS DÉCLASSÉ.
MAN, I TOTALLY SURFED THAT 'LANCHE!	I WAS NEARLY KILLED BY AN AVALANCHE TODAY!
BOGUS! MY DEW'S BEEN BREACHED.	GRACIOUS! SOMEONE DRANK MY SODA.
I HAVE TO BLAST A DOOKIE.	I HAVE TO GO TO THE BATHROOM.
WOW, THAT CHICK DID A TIGHT! WHO IS SHE?	I AM ENAMORED OF THAT WOMAN'S SNOW RODEO. PERHAPS I WILL TALK TO HER.
DUDE! CHECK IT!	PAY ATTENTION TO ME, GOOD FRIEND, FOR I AM AN EXPERT SNOWBOARDER, AND IF YOU DON'T LOOK, MY AMAZING TRICK WILL BE HISTORY, JUST LIKE SANDS THROUGH AN HOURGLASS LOST IN THE WINDS OF TIME.

HOLIDAY ENTERTAINMENT

	8:00 PM	8:30 PM	9:00 PM
OY!	TV MOVIE – *HERSCHEL, THE HANUKKAH BOOKIE* - Krusty the Clown stars in this holiday tale of a bookie with a heart of gelt.		
PRY	SPECIAL REPORT – **SANTA CLAUS, BELOVED ALTRUIST OR MERCILESS CORPORATE TYRANT?** A profile by fellow merciless corporate tyrant C. Montgomery Burns.		**TO BE ANNOUNCED** - Filler
¡EH!	ESPECIAL – *UNA NAVIDADA MUY DEPLORABLE* para Bumblebee Man. ¡Que lastima!		
HICK	MOVIE – *NORTH POLE COUNTY LINE* – Kris Kringle takes up running moonshine in the off season.		
BRAT	*POOCHIE SAVES CHRISTMAS* Annoyingly extreme dog helps Santa deliver presents.	*ITCHY & SCRATCHY'S BLOODY NEW YEAR* Lovable cat and mouse team up to murder annoyingly extreme dog.	
GLUT	**YULETIDE YUMMIES** Fruitcake, eggnog, and plum pudding.	**HANUKKAH NOSH** – Latkes, rugalah, and soufganiyot.	
YAWN	**LOCAL PUBLIC ACCESS** – Concerned churchgoer Ned Flanders on the True Meaning of Christmas (NOTE: May be preempted by test pattern).		
D'OH!	**SPRINGFIELD'S FUNNIEST DECORATING DISASTERS MARATHON** Candid footage of local oaf and father of three electrocuting self while hanging holiday lights.		

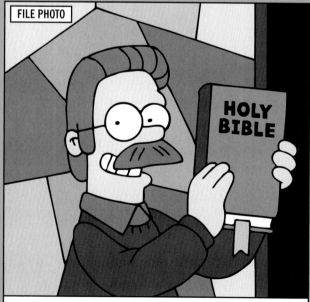

FILE PHOTO

HOLY BIBLE

YAWN (8:00PM)
Concerned churchgoer Ned Flanders on the True Meaning of Christmas

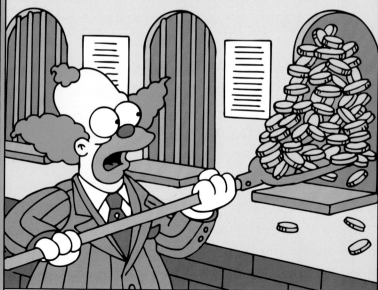

OY! (8:00PM)
TV MOVIE – *HERSCHEL, THE HANUKKAH BOOKIE*

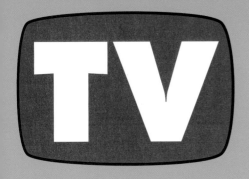

TV LISTINGS

9:30 PM	10:00 PM
OH, THOSE MACCABEES! (sitcom) Yehudit goes on the warpath when Judah leaves the holy oil at the office.	
SPECIAL REPORT — Kent Brockman investigates: "EGGNOG, Beverage of Death?"	
	PARA SER ANNUNCIADO - PAP
LURLEEN LUMPKIN'S DOWN-HOME OL' FASHIONED TRAILER PARK CHRISTMAS — **IN REHAB** — with special guest stars Buck McCoy and the Ya Hoo Recovering Alcoholic Jug Band.	
TV MOVIE - *ON, PLOPPER!* Original holiday tale of incontinent pig longing to join Santa's reindeer team.	
LARD BUSTERS — Remorse, shame, and regret.	
DEBATE — Ned Flanders takes on the Costington's Santa Claus.	
SPRINGFIELD'S FUNNIEST DECORATING DISASTERS MARATHON The fun continues at Springfield General Hospital.	

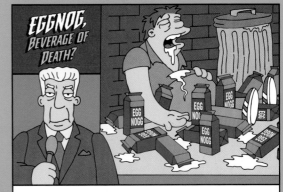

PRY (9:30PM) SPECIAL REPORT

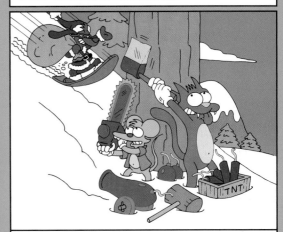

BRAT (8:30PM) ITCHY & SCRATCHY SPECIAL

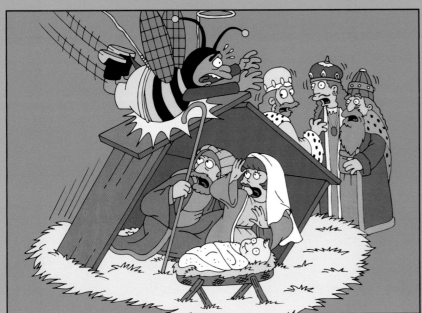

¡EH! (8:00PM)
ESPECIAL – *UNA NAVIDADA MUY DEPLORABLE*

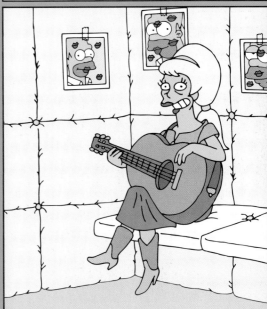

HICK (9:30PM) LURLEEN LUMPKIN'S DOWN-HOME
OL' FASHIONED TRAILER PARK CHRISTMAS — IN REHAB

HOT CIDER IN THE CITY

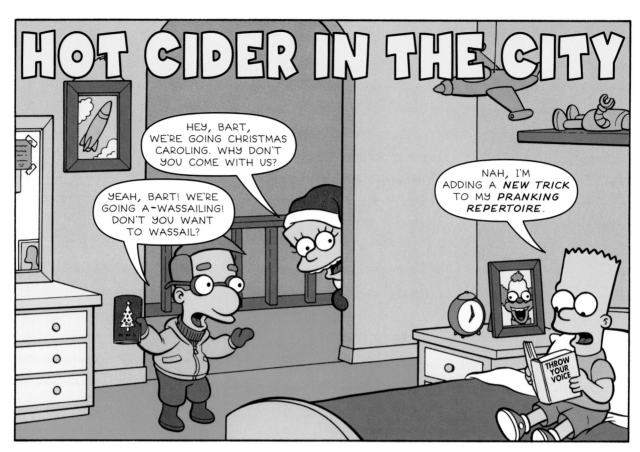

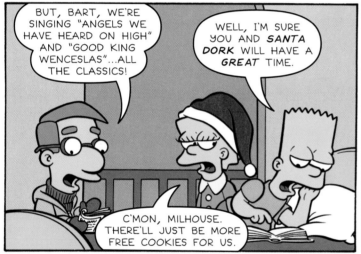

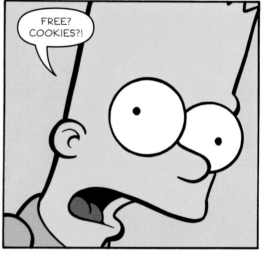

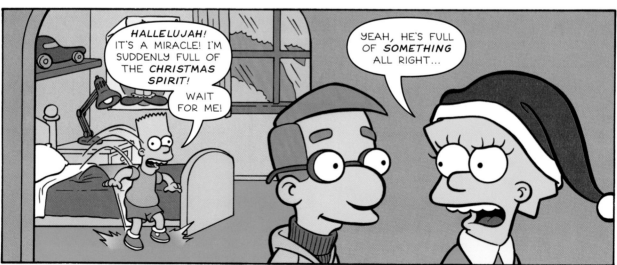

TONY DIGEROLAMO
SCRIPT

JASON HO
PENCILS

ANDREW PEPOY
INKS

NATHAN KANE
COLORS

KAREN BATES
LETTERS

BILL MORRISON
EDITOR

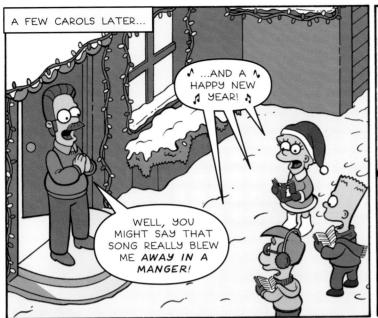

A FEW CAROLS LATER...

♪ ...AND A ♪ HAPPY NEW ♪ YEAR! ♪

WELL, YOU MIGHT SAY THAT SONG REALLY BLEW ME *AWAY IN A MANGER!*

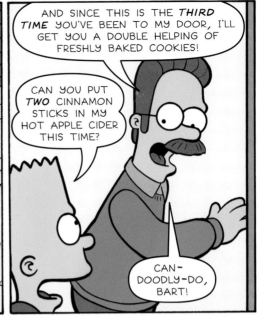

AND SINCE THIS IS THE *THIRD TIME* YOU'VE BEEN TO MY DOOR, I'LL GET YOU A DOUBLE HELPING OF FRESHLY BAKED COOKIES!

CAN YOU PUT *TWO* CINNAMON STICKS IN MY HOT APPLE CIDER THIS TIME?

CAN-DOODLY-DO, BART!

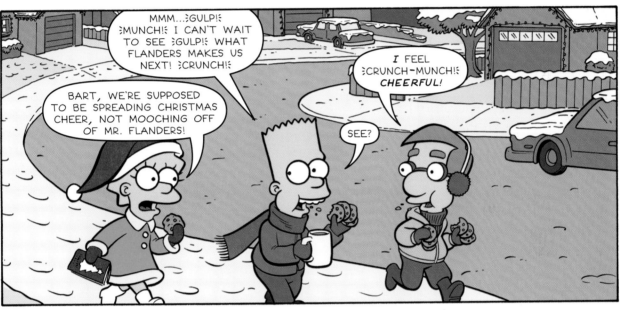

MMM...≷GULP!≷ ≷MUNCH!≷ I CAN'T WAIT TO SEE ≷GULP!≷ WHAT FLANDERS MAKES US NEXT! ≷CRUNCH!≷

BART, WE'RE SUPPOSED TO BE SPREADING CHRISTMAS CHEER, NOT MOOCHING OFF OF MR. FLANDERS!

I FEEL ≷CRUNCH-MUNCH!≷ *CHEERFUL!*

SEE?

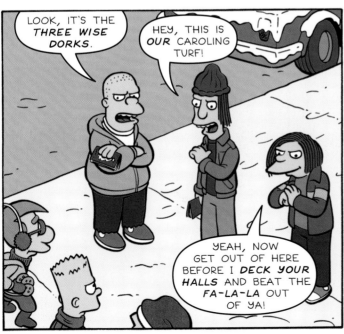

LOOK, IT'S THE *THREE WISE DORKS.*

HEY, THIS IS *OUR* CAROLING TURF!

YEAH, NOW GET OUT OF HERE BEFORE I *DECK YOUR HALLS* AND BEAT THE *FA-LA-LA* OUT OF YA!

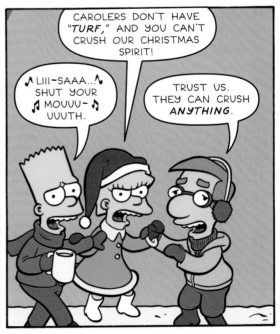

CAROLERS DON'T HAVE *"TURF,"* AND YOU CAN'T CRUSH OUR CHRISTMAS SPIRIT!

♪ LIII-SAAA...♪ SHUT YOUR ♪ MOUUU-♪ UUUTH.

TRUST US. THEY CAN CRUSH *ANYTHING.*

WE'RE TAKIN' OVER YOUR ROUTE, SIMPSON. NOW WHICH HOUSE IS GIVIN' OUT THE CINNAMON STICKS?
NO, BART, DON'T TELL THEM!
LISA, I DON'T THINK I HAVE A CHOICE.
ONE SEASON'S BEATING LATER...
YOU BULLIES AREN'T GOING TO GET AWAY WITH THIS! THIS IS **ANTI-CHRISTMAS!**
HA HA HA HA!
THE ONLY THING YOU'RE GOING TO GET FOR CHRISTMAS IS A LUMP OF COAL IN YOUR STOCKINGS!
OW!
WELL, I GUESS I SHOULD'VE SEEN ***THAT*** COMING.
OH, BART, NOW WE CAN'T CAROL ANYWHERE. I'M SORRY WE DRAGGED YOU ALONG FOR THIS.
LIS, I'M ABOUT TO GIVE YOU AN EARLY CHRISTMAS PRESENT.
"I DIDN'T SEND THEM TO FLANDERS' HOUSE..."
♪ SILVER BELLS...SILVER BELLS...IT'S CHRISTMAS TIME IN THE CITY... ♪

CHRISTMAS CAROLS FOR ME? SNIFF! NOBODY'S EVER SUNG ME NUTHIN' BEFORE. I THINK I'M GONNA CRY LIKE A WOMAN HERE.
TING-A-LING...
WATCH ME THROW MY VOICE...
THIS IS TO MAKE UP FOR ALL THE PRANK PHONE CALLS DURING THE YEAR!
WHUH--? THAT WAS YOU?!
HEAR THEM RING...
C'MERE, YOU ROTTEN BRATS! ALL YOU'RE GONNA WANT FOR CHRISTMAS IS YOUR TWO FRONT TEETH AND A NEW SPLEEN WHEN I GET DONE WITH YOU!
AAAAAH!
BART, I THINK YOUR PLAN LACKED THE PROPER CHRISTMAS CHEER.
SO IT'S CHRISTMAS CHEER YOU WANT, EH?
LAST ONE BACK TO FLANDERS' HOUSE IS A ROTTEN ELF!
JOYEUX NOEL!

Christmas Eve at
Duff BEER
MAY
TO: MAGGIE
FROM: UNCLE MOE

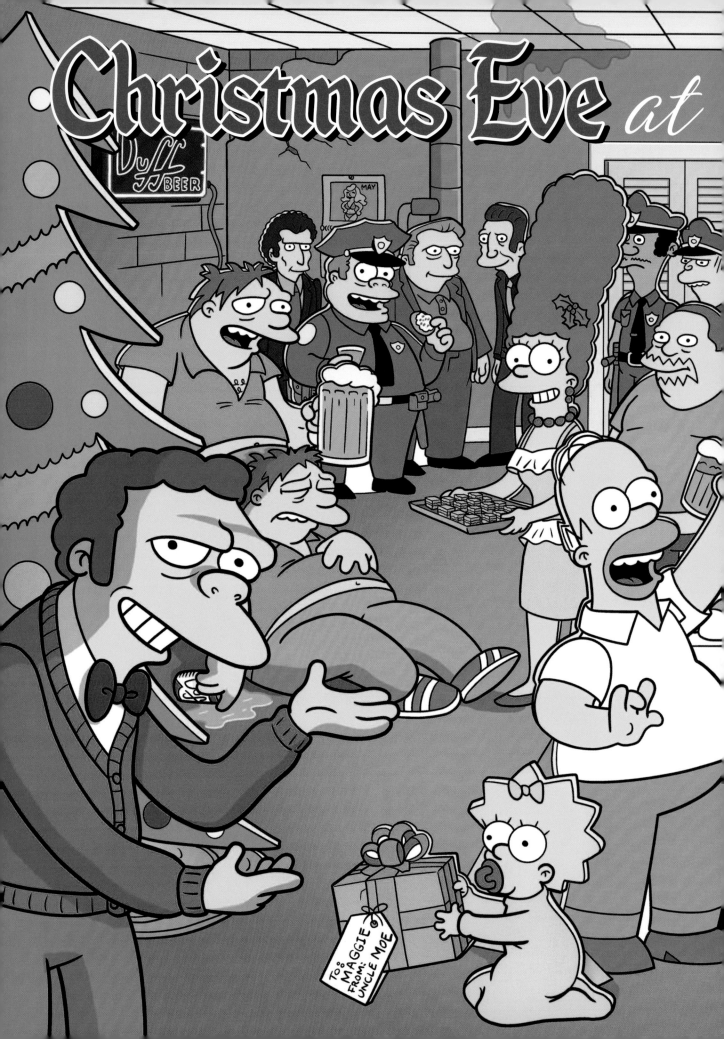

Casa Szyslak
MAYOR

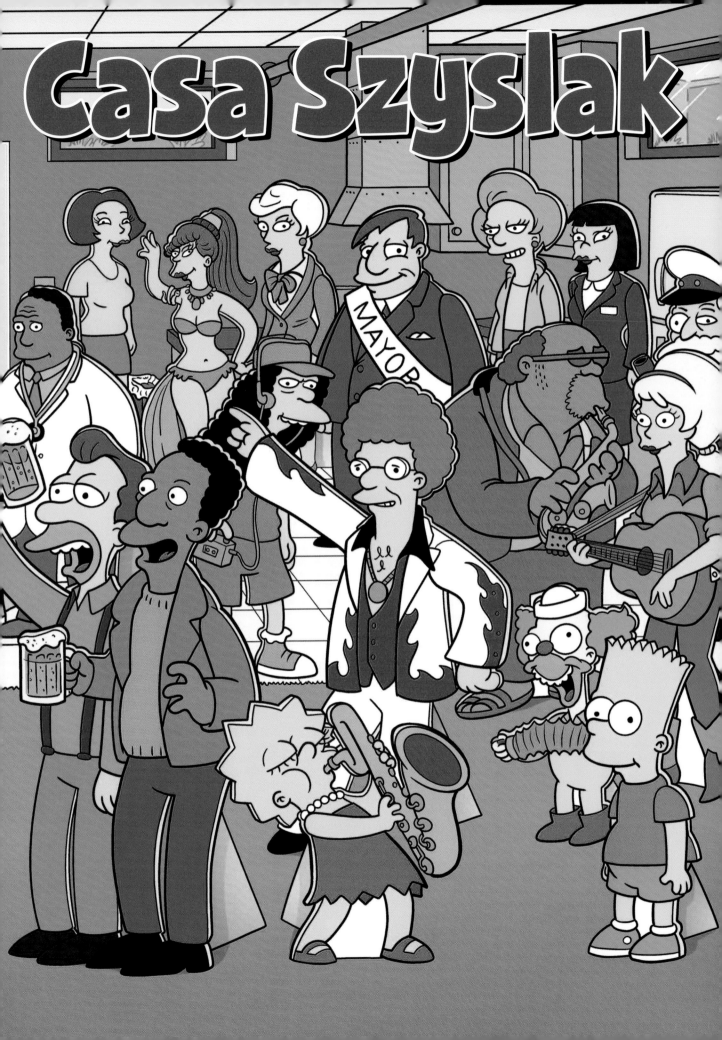

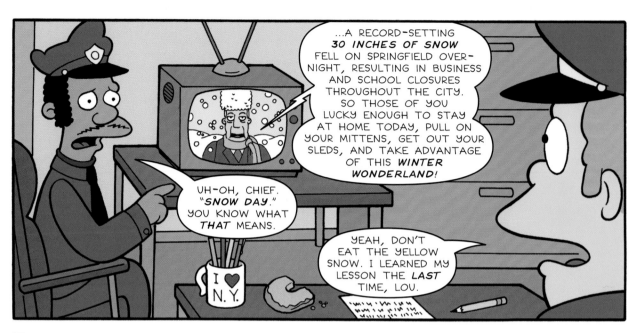

...A RECORD-SETTING **30 INCHES OF SNOW** FELL ON SPRINGFIELD OVERNIGHT, RESULTING IN BUSINESS AND SCHOOL CLOSURES THROUGHOUT THE CITY. SO THOSE OF YOU LUCKY ENOUGH TO STAY AT HOME TODAY, PULL ON YOUR MITTENS, GET OUT YOUR SLEDS, AND TAKE ADVANTAGE OF THIS **WINTER WONDERLAND!**

UH-OH, CHIEF. "**SNOW DAY**." YOU KNOW WHAT **THAT** MEANS.

YEAH, DON'T EAT THE YELLOW SNOW. I LEARNED MY LESSON THE **LAST** TIME, LOU.

I ♥ N.Y.

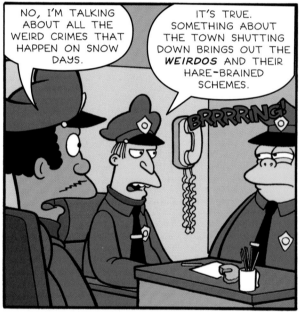

NO, I'M TALKING ABOUT ALL THE WEIRD CRIMES THAT HAPPEN ON SNOW DAYS.

IT'S TRUE. SOMETHING ABOUT THE TOWN SHUTTING DOWN BRINGS OUT THE **WEIRDOS** AND THEIR HARE-BRAINED SCHEMES.

BRRRRING!

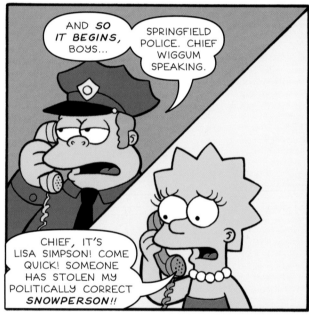

AND **SO IT BEGINS,** BOYS...

SPRINGFIELD POLICE. CHIEF WIGGUM SPEAKING.

CHIEF, IT'S LISA SIMPSON! COME QUICK! SOMEONE HAS STOLEN MY POLITICALLY CORRECT **SNOWPERSON**!!

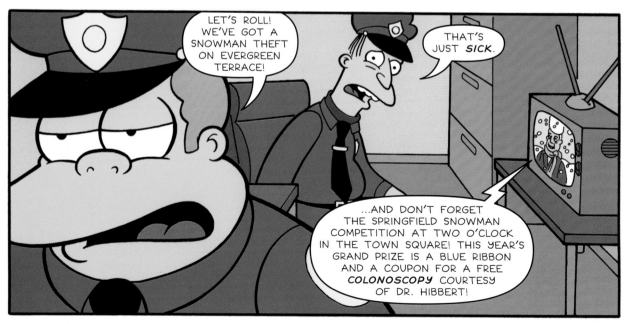

LET'S ROLL! WE'VE GOT A SNOWMAN THEFT ON EVERGREEN TERRACE!

THAT'S JUST **SICK**.

...AND DON'T FORGET THE SPRINGFIELD SNOWMAN COMPETITION AT TWO O'CLOCK IN THE TOWN SQUARE! THIS YEAR'S GRAND PRIZE IS A BLUE RIBBON AND A COUPON FOR A FREE **COLONOSCOPY** COURTESY OF DR. HIBBERT!

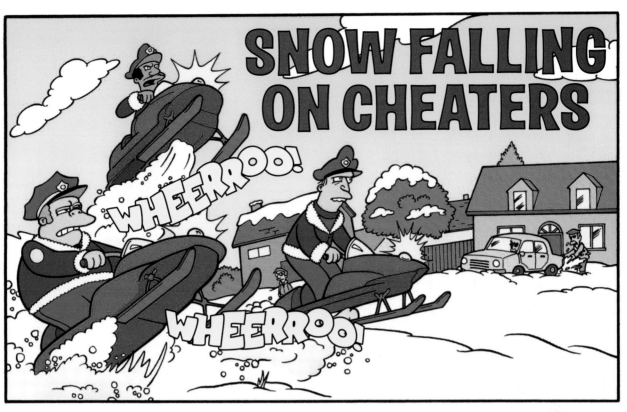

SNOW FALLING ON CHEATERS

WHEERROO!

WHEERROO!

WHEERROO!

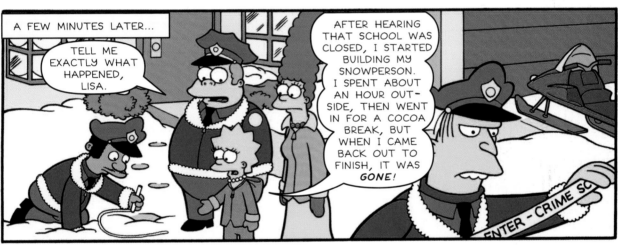

A FEW MINUTES LATER...

TELL ME EXACTLY WHAT HAPPENED, LISA.

AFTER HEARING THAT SCHOOL WAS CLOSED, I STARTED BUILDING MY SNOWPERSON. I SPENT ABOUT AN HOUR OUTSIDE, THEN WENT IN FOR A COCOA BREAK, BUT WHEN I CAME BACK OUT TO FINISH, IT WAS *GONE!*

ENTER - CRIME SC

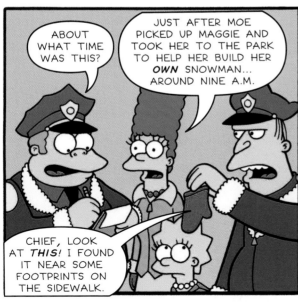

ABOUT WHAT TIME WAS THIS?

JUST AFTER MOE PICKED UP MAGGIE AND TOOK HER TO THE PARK TO HELP HER BUILD HER *OWN* SNOWMAN... AROUND NINE A.M.

CHIEF, LOOK AT *THIS!* I FOUND IT NEAR SOME FOOTPRINTS ON THE SIDEWALK.

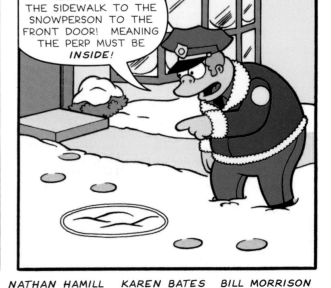

THEY LEAD FROM THE SIDEWALK TO THE SNOWPERSON TO THE FRONT DOOR! MEANING THE PERP MUST BE *INSIDE!*

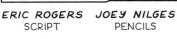

ERIC ROGERS
SCRIPT

JOEY NILGES
PENCILS

MIKE DECARLO
INKS

NATHAN HAMILL
COLORS

KAREN BATES
LETTERS

BILL MORRISON
EDITOR

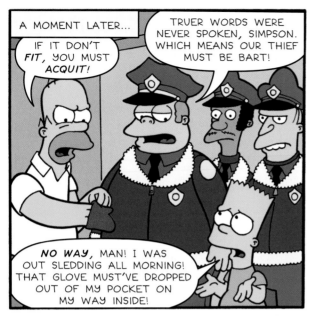

A MOMENT LATER...

IF IT DON'T *FIT*, YOU MUST *ACQUIT!*

TRUER WORDS WERE NEVER SPOKEN, SIMPSON. WHICH MEANS OUR THIEF MUST BE BART!

NO WAY, MAN! I WAS OUT SLEDDING ALL MORNING! THAT GLOVE MUST'VE DROPPED OUT OF MY POCKET ON MY WAY INSIDE!

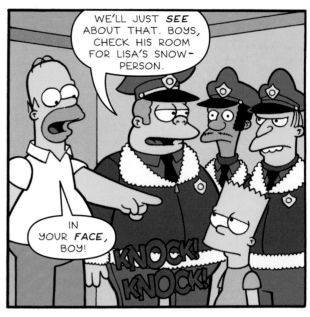

WE'LL JUST *SEE* ABOUT THAT. BOYS, CHECK HIS ROOM FOR LISA'S SNOW-PERSON.

IN YOUR *FACE*, BOY!

KNOCK! KNOCK!

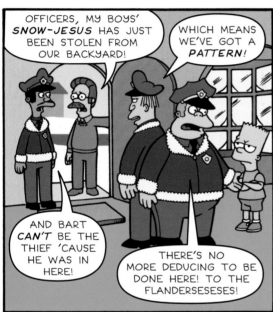

OFFICERS, MY BOYS' *SNOW-JESUS* HAS JUST BEEN STOLEN FROM OUR BACKYARD!

WHICH MEANS WE'VE GOT A *PATTERN!*

AND BART *CAN'T* BE THE THIEF 'CAUSE HE WAS IN HERE!

THERE'S NO MORE DEDUCING TO BE DONE HERE! TO THE FLANDERSESESES!

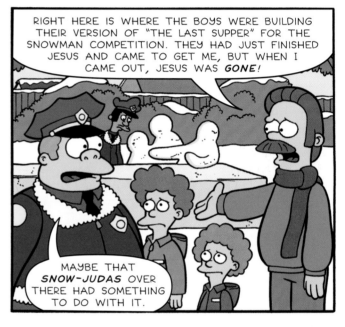

RIGHT HERE IS WHERE THE BOYS WERE BUILDING THEIR VERSION OF "THE LAST SUPPER" FOR THE SNOWMAN COMPETITION. THEY HAD JUST FINISHED JESUS AND CAME TO GET ME, BUT WHEN I CAME OUT, JESUS WAS *GONE!*

MAYBE THAT *SNOW-JUDAS* OVER THERE HAD SOMETHING TO DO WITH IT.

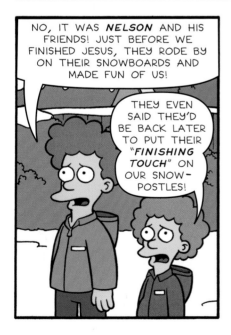

NO, IT WAS *NELSON* AND HIS FRIENDS! JUST BEFORE WE FINISHED JESUS, THEY RODE BY ON THEIR SNOWBOARDS AND MADE FUN OF US!

THEY EVEN SAID THEY'D BE BACK LATER TO PUT THEIR *"FINISHING TOUCH"* ON OUR SNOW-POSTLES!

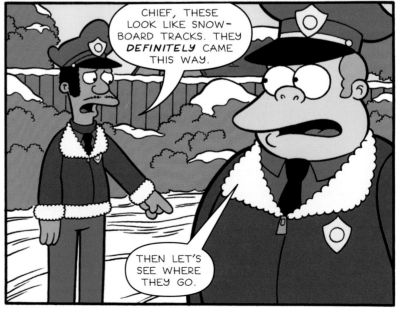

CHIEF, THESE LOOK LIKE SNOW-BOARD TRACKS. THEY *DEFINITELY* CAME THIS WAY.

THEN LET'S SEE WHERE THEY GO.

AT THE KWIK-E-MART...

...SO YOU'RE SAYING YOU *DIDN'T* TOUCH THE SNOW-JESUS OR LISA'S SNOWPERSON?

JACK POT · PLAY to WIN HERE.

Duff BEER 36 pack $12.9

FOR THE LAST TIME, DUDE, WE DIDN'T TAKE ANY STUPID SNOWMEN!

AND IF WE HAD, WHERE WOULD WE *HIDE* THEM?

AND HOW WOULD WE *CARRY THEM* ON OUR SNOWBOARDS?

HEY! IF ANYONE'S GONNA ASK THE *STUPID QUESTIONS* AROUND HERE, IT'S GONNA BE *ME*!

I STILL SAY WE TAKE 'EM IN FOR QUESTIONING, CHIEF.

OFFICERS, I BELIEVE YOU ARE BARKING UP THE *WRONG SKIRT*!

WHY'S THAT?

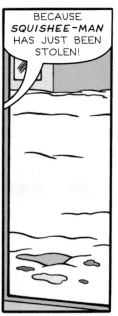

BECAUSE *SQUISHEE-MAN* HAS JUST BEEN STOLEN!

SQUISHEE-MAN?

MY ENTRY INTO THE SNOWMAN COMPETITION! I MADE HIM FROM SNOW AND SQUISHEE. HE'S THE SNOWMAN YOU CAN *EAT* AFTER YOU GROW BORED OF HIS NOTHINGNESS!

SQUISHEE-MAN WAS THERE WHEN WE CAME IN, CHIEF.

WHICH MEANS ONE OF YOUR MOST RECENT CUSTOMERS MUST HAVE TAKEN HIM!

HE MUST HAVE DONE THIS PERPETRATION!

LET'S SHRED!!!

VRROOOMM!

PULL OVER!
GNARLY!
WHEERROO! WHEERROO!
IS THERE, LIKE, SOMETHING TOTALLY WRONG, OFFICER DUDE?
I NEED TO CHECK THIS VEHICLE FOR STOLEN SNOW-MEN, SIR.
NO SNOWMEN HERE, DUDE!
SO THERE AREN'T. BUT I WOULD ADVISE YOU TO WEAR THAT SKI MASK--IT'S TOO COLD OUT HERE NOT TO!
FOR SURE!
CHIEF, WE JUST GOT A CALL! THERE'S BEEN ANOTHER SNOWMAN STOLEN FROM THE DUFF FACTORY!
LET'S GO!
DUFFMAN WAS BUILDING TWO PUMPED-UP DUFF SNOW GIRLS FOR THE SNOWMAN COMPETITION! OH YEAH!
BUT WHEN DUFFMAN HAD TO GO INSIDE FOR A TOTALLY AWESOME POTTY BREAK, SOME-ONE STOLE HIS MASTERPIECE!
ANY IDEA WHO DID IT?
MAYBE IT WAS FAT TONY AND HIS GANG. THEY LEANED ON DUFFMAN AND TOLD HIM THEY PLAN TO MUSCLE IN ON THE BEER BUSINESS WITH THE NEW BREW "GOOM-BEER."
WE'RE GETTING CLOSER AND CLOSER, BOYS...
TO SOLVING THE CASE, CHIEF?
NO, TO THE END OF THE DAY, WHEN WE CAN GO HOME. WE MIGHT AS WELL QUESTION FAT TONY AND HIS CREW FIRST.

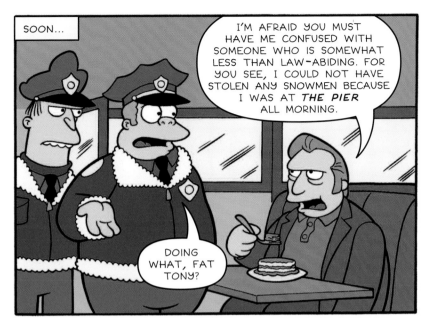

SOON...

I'M AFRAID YOU MUST HAVE ME CONFUSED WITH SOMEONE WHO IS SOMEWHAT LESS THAN LAW-ABIDING. FOR YOU SEE, I COULD NOT HAVE STOLEN ANY SNOWMEN BECAUSE I WAS AT *THE PIER* ALL MORNING.

DOING WHAT, FAT TONY?

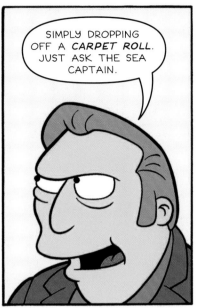

SIMPLY DROPPING OFF A *CARPET ROLL*. JUST ASK THE SEA CAPTAIN.

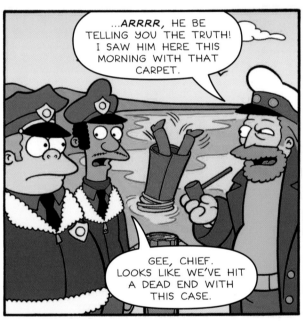

...*ARRRR*, HE BE TELLING YOU THE TRUTH! I SAW HIM HERE THIS MORNING WITH THAT CARPET.

GEE, CHIEF. LOOKS LIKE WE'VE HIT A DEAD END WITH THIS CASE.

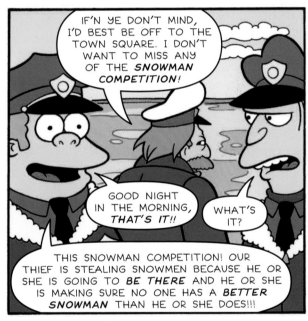

IF'N YE DON'T MIND, I'D BEST BE OFF TO THE TOWN SQUARE. I DON'T WANT TO MISS ANY OF THE *SNOWMAN COMPETITION*!

GOOD NIGHT IN THE MORNING, *THAT'S IT!!*

WHAT'S IT?

THIS SNOWMAN COMPETITION! OUR THIEF IS STEALING SNOWMEN BECAUSE HE OR SHE IS GOING TO *BE THERE* AND HE OR SHE IS MAKING SURE NO ONE HAS A *BETTER SNOWMAN* THAN HE OR SHE DOES!!!

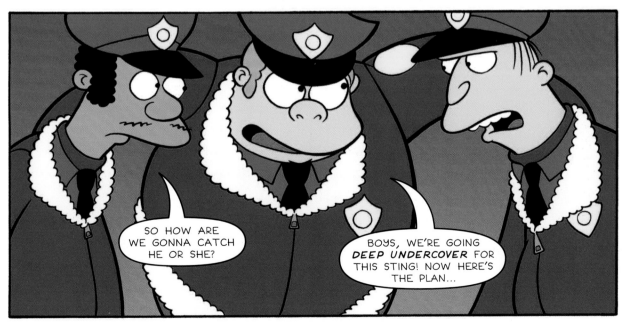

SO HOW ARE WE GONNA CATCH HE OR SHE?

BOYS, WE'RE GOING *DEEP UNDERCOVER* FOR THIS STING! NOW HERE'S THE PLAN...

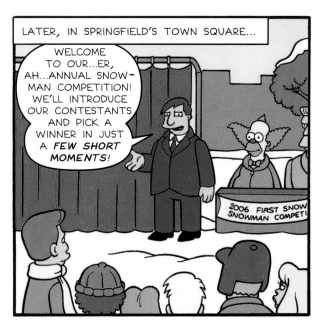

LATER, IN SPRINGFIELD'S TOWN SQUARE...

WELCOME TO OUR...ER, AH...ANNUAL SNOW-MAN COMPETITION! WE'LL INTRODUCE OUR CONTESTANTS AND PICK A WINNER IN JUST A *FEW SHORT MOMENTS!*

2006 FIRST SNOW SNOWMAN COMPETI

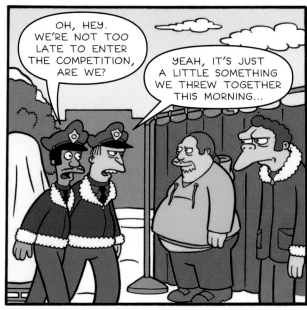

OH, HEY. WE'RE NOT TOO LATE TO ENTER THE COMPETITION, ARE WE?

YEAH, IT'S JUST A LITTLE SOMETHING WE THREW TOGETHER THIS MORNING...

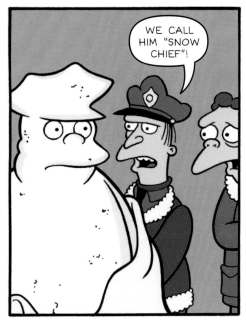

WE CALL HIM "SNOW CHIEF"!

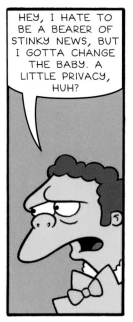

HEY, I HATE TO BE A BEARER OF STINKY NEWS, BUT I GOTTA CHANGE THE BABY. A LITTLE PRIVACY, HUH?

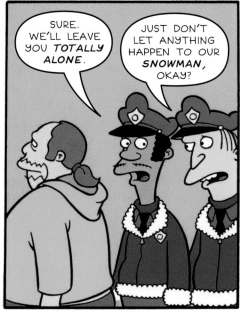

SURE. WE'LL LEAVE YOU *TOTALLY ALONE.*

JUST DON'T LET ANYTHING HAPPEN TO OUR *SNOWMAN,* OKAY?

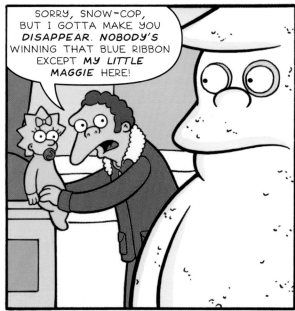

SORRY, SNOW-COP, BUT I GOTTA MAKE YOU *DISAPPEAR. NOBODY'S* WINNING THAT BLUE RIBBON EXCEPT *MY LITTLE MAGGIE* HERE!

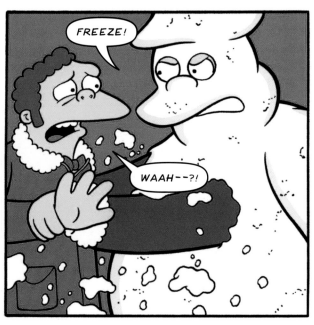

FREEZE!

WAAH--?!

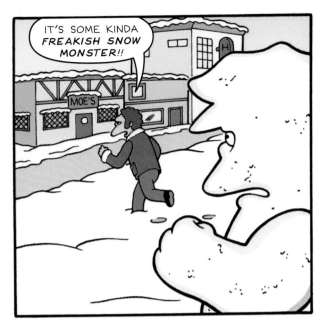

IT'S SOME KINDA *FREAKISH SNOW MONSTER!!*

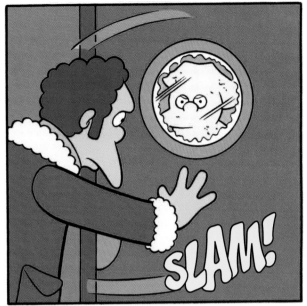

SLAM!

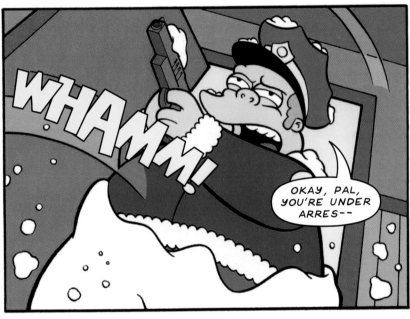

WHAMM!

OKAY, PAL, YOU'RE UNDER ARRES--

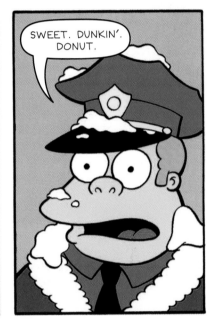

SWEET. DUNKIN'. DONUT.

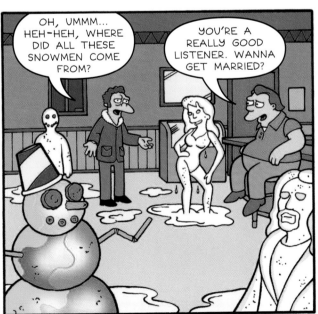

OH, UMMM... HEH-HEH, WHERE DID ALL THESE SNOWMEN COME FROM?

YOU'RE A REALLY GOOD LISTENER. WANNA GET MARRIED?

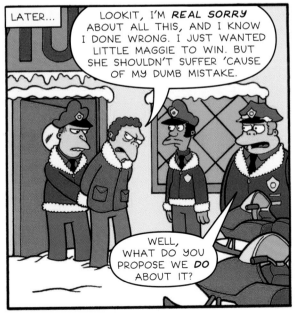

LATER...

LOOKIT, I'M *REAL SORRY* ABOUT ALL THIS, AND I KNOW I DONE WRONG. I JUST WANTED LITTLE MAGGIE TO WIN. BUT SHE SHOULDN'T SUFFER 'CAUSE OF MY DUMB MISTAKE.

WELL, WHAT DO YOU PROPOSE WE *DO* ABOUT IT?

A LITTLE LATER, IN THE MIDDLE OF TOWN...
WELL THEN, WITHOUT ANY FURTHER DELAY, LET'S SEE OUR SNOWMEN!!
THIS IS THE ONLY ONE??
SIGH I GUESS HE'S THE WINNER THEN.
WAIT!!
I CALL IT "CRAZY, SEXY, COOL: A SELF-PORTRAIT."
I BRAKE for TAUNTAUNS
THIS IS MAGGIE'S ENTRY!
NOW THAT'S A SNOWMAN!
THE WINNER... ER, AH...IS MAGGIE SIMPSON!
WORST. LAST-MINUTE ENTRY. EVER!
I JUST KNEW SHE'D WIN!
AT LAST, CECIL, WE'VE FINALLY DUG OUR WAY OUT OF PRISON! AND JUST LOOK--UNATTENDED SNOWMOBILES FOR OUR GETAWAY!
HOW FORTUITOUS!
UH-OH. THIS AIN'T GOOD...
THE END

YES, FLANDERS, THERE IS A SANTA CLAUS
KWIK-E-MART
Merry X-MAS
JACK POT PLAY TO WIN HERE!
MILK. EGGS. GROUND BEEF...
Duff Beer SUITCASE 12.95

JAMES W. BATES SCRIPT | JEREMY ROBINSON PENCILS | SHANE GLINES INKS | ROBERT STANLEY COLORS | KAREN BATES LETTERS | BILL MORRISON EDITOR

HAPPY HOLIDAYS, MISTER REVEREND!
HAPPY *CHRISTMAS*, APU!
HO HO!
X-MA
X-MAS CANES
MATT GROENING

Merry Squishmas
MERRY *SQUISHMAS*?
X-MAS RED
X-MAS GREEN
KWIK-E BEEF
MEATS
Chicken...

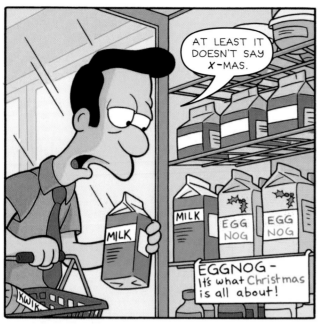

AT LEAST IT DOESN'T SAY *X*-MAS.

MILK

MILK   EGG NOG   EGG NOG

EGGNOG — It's what Christmas is all about!

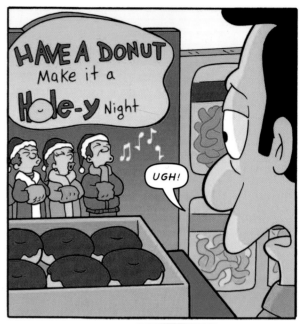

HAVE A DONUT Make it a Hole-y Night

UGH!

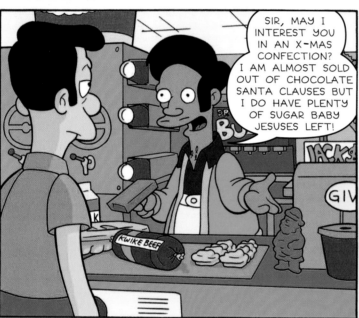

SIR, MAY I INTEREST YOU IN AN X-MAS CONFECTION? I AM ALMOST SOLD OUT OF CHOCOLATE SANTA CLAUSES BUT I DO HAVE PLENTY OF SUGAR BABY JESUSES LEFT!

KWIKE BEEF

GIV

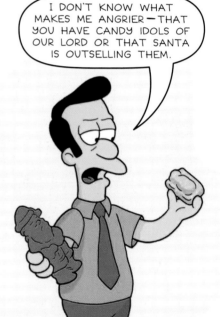

I DON'T KNOW WHAT MAKES ME ANGRIER — THAT YOU HAVE CANDY IDOLS OF OUR LORD OR THAT SANTA IS OUTSELLING THEM.

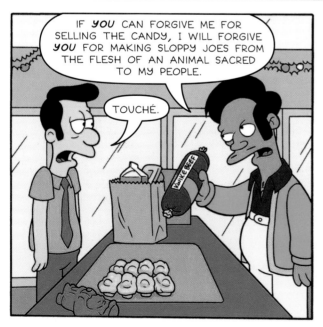

IF *YOU* CAN FORGIVE ME FOR SELLING THE CANDY, I WILL FORGIVE *YOU* FOR MAKING SLOPPY JOES FROM THE FLESH OF AN ANIMAL SACRED TO MY PEOPLE.

TOUCHÉ.

KWIKE BEEF

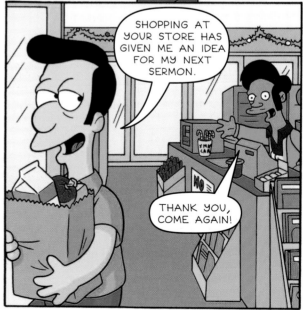

SHOPPING AT YOUR STORE HAS GIVEN ME AN IDEA FOR MY NEXT SERMON.

THANK YOU, COME AGAIN!

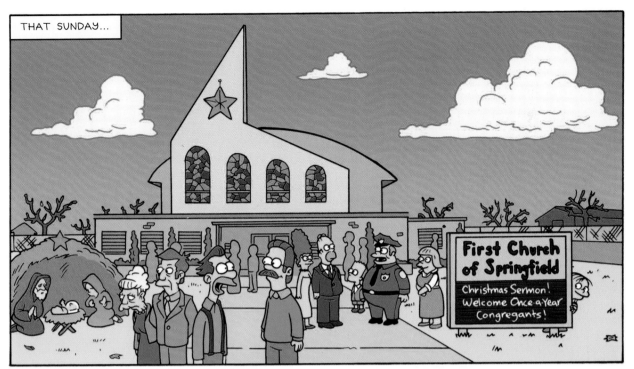

THAT SUNDAY...

First Church of Springfield

Christmas Sermon!
Welcome Once-a-Year Congregants!

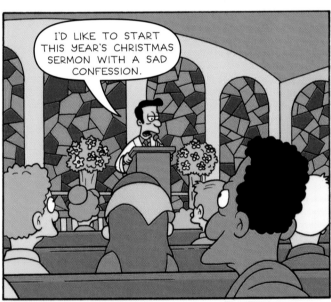

I'D LIKE TO START THIS YEAR'S CHRISTMAS SERMON WITH A SAD CONFESSION.

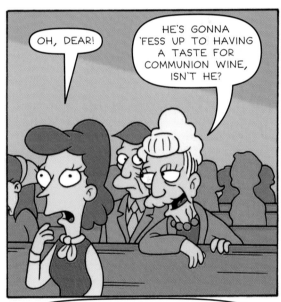

OH, DEAR!

HE'S GONNA 'FESS UP TO HAVING A TASTE FOR COMMUNION WINE, ISN'T HE?

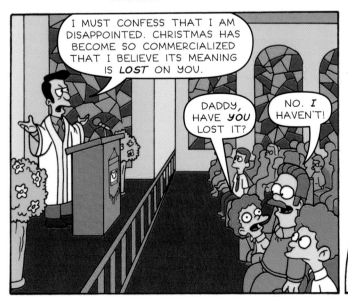

I MUST CONFESS THAT I AM DISAPPOINTED. CHRISTMAS HAS BECOME SO COMMERCIALIZED THAT I BELIEVE ITS MEANING IS *LOST* ON YOU.

DADDY, HAVE *YOU* LOST IT?

NO. *I* HAVEN'T!

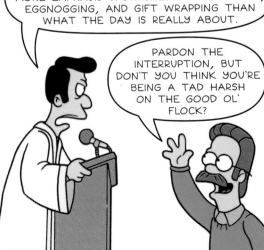

YOU PEOPLE MARGINALIZE CHRISTMAS MORE AND MORE EVERY YEAR. YOU PUT MORE EMPHASIS UPON CHESTNUT ROASTING, EGGNOGGING, AND GIFT WRAPPING THAN WHAT THE DAY IS REALLY ABOUT.

PARDON THE INTERRUPTION, BUT DON'T YOU THINK YOU'RE BEING A TAD HARSH ON THE GOOD OL' FLOCK?

89

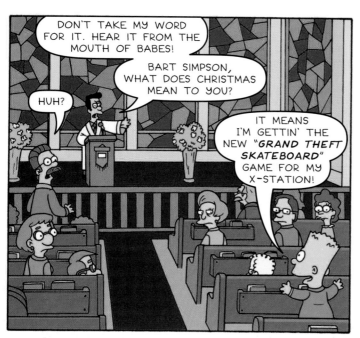

DON'T TAKE MY WORD FOR IT. HEAR IT FROM THE MOUTH OF BABES!

BART SIMPSON, WHAT DOES CHRISTMAS MEAN TO YOU?

HUH?

IT MEANS I'M GETTIN' THE NEW "GRAND THEFT SKATEBOARD" GAME FOR MY X-STATION!

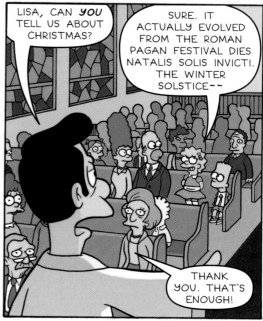

LISA, CAN YOU TELL US ABOUT CHRISTMAS?

SURE. IT ACTUALLY EVOLVED FROM THE ROMAN PAGAN FESTIVAL DIES NATALIS SOLIS INVICTI. THE WINTER SOLSTICE--

THANK YOU. THAT'S ENOUGH!

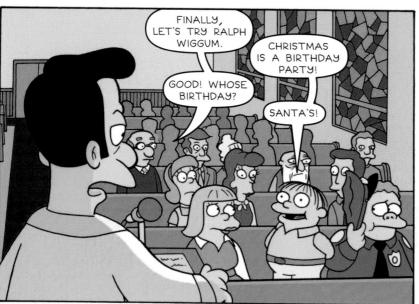

FINALLY, LET'S TRY RALPH WIGGUM.

CHRISTMAS IS A BIRTHDAY PARTY!

GOOD! WHOSE BIRTHDAY?

SANTA'S!

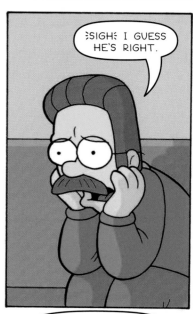

ᴇSIGHᴇ I GUESS HE'S RIGHT.

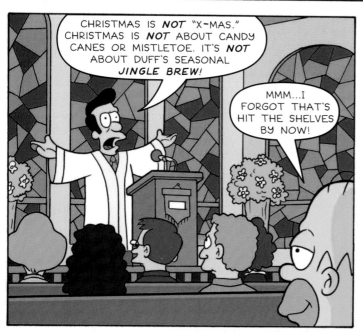

CHRISTMAS IS NOT "X-MAS." CHRISTMAS IS NOT ABOUT CANDY CANES OR MISTLETOE. IT'S NOT ABOUT DUFF'S SEASONAL JINGLE BREW!

MMM...I FORGOT THAT'S HIT THE SHELVES BY NOW!

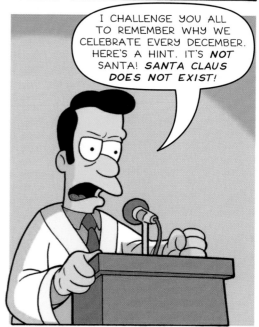

I CHALLENGE YOU ALL TO REMEMBER WHY WE CELEBRATE EVERY DECEMBER. HERE'S A HINT. IT'S NOT SANTA! SANTA CLAUS DOES NOT EXIST!

A LITTLE BIT LATER...
GOD BLESS ICE CREAM!
AMEN, HOMER! MAKE THIS "ICE CREAM AFTER CHURCH" DEAL PERMANENT, AND I'LL BECOME A CHOIRBOY.
WHY **DID** WE GO FOR ICE CREAM?
I THOUGHT IT WOULD BE A NICE TREAT.
AND...?
I ALSO THOUGHT IT WOULD SOOTHE ANY FRAYED NERVES CAUSED BY WHAT REVEREND LOVEJOY SAID ABOUT SANTA.
WE'RE NOT LITTLE KIDS. WE **KNOW** THE TRUTH.
YEAH! A FAT MAN IS GETTING ME THE "GRAND THEFT SKATEBOARD" GAME, BUT I **KNOW** IT AIN'T SANTA.
OOF!
I **DO** WORRY ABOUT ROD AND TODD!
NED DID GET A LITTLE HOT UNDER THE COLLAR.
STUPID HOT-COLLAR FLANDERS.

HEY, GUYS, WHAT ARE YOU DOING?
PUTTING OUT THE TRASH.
YOU'RE THROWING OUT CHRISTMAS DECORATIONS?
THE REVEREND SAID WE'VE MADE CHRISTMAS INTO A COMMERCIAL, SO DADDY WANTS ALL THIS STUFF GONE.
DADDY SAYS SANTA DOESN'T EXIST.
WHY ARE YOU CHUCKING THE THANKSGIVING STUFF?
DADDY DIDN'T WANT TO TAKE ANY CHANCES.
BOYS, LET'S GET A MOO-DIDDLY-OOVE ON. THERE'S STILL TINSEL TO BE SHREDDED!
SIGH!
I LIKED SANTA.
C'MON, TODD. WE'VE GOT HALLS TO UNDECK.

WEIRD. SEEING THE GOOFBALLS SAD BUMS ME OUT.
THAT'S CALLED EMPATHY.
WHATEVER. IT STINKS THAT MR. FLANDERS HAS TAKEN THE LAST TRAIN TO GRINCHVILLE.
THE HOLIDAY HAS BEEN COMMERCIALIZED, BUT I WISH REVEREND LOVEJOY DIDN'T FEEL LIKE HE HAD TO TAKE SANTA AWAY.
I KNOW! CHRISTMAS IS GOING TO BE RUINED FOR ROD AND TODD.
IT'S LIKE WHEN I EXPLAINED TO YOU THAT PRO WRESTLING WAS FAKE.
IS NOT!
UGH.
HEY, WHAT IF WE BRING SANTY BACK?
UH-OH. I KNOW THAT DEVIOUS LOOK.
YES, BUT THIS TIME I'LL USE MY EVIL GENIUS FOR GOOD!
WHAT ARE YOU SUGGESTING?
I'M SAYING WE SHOULD BE SANTA FOR ROD AND TODD.

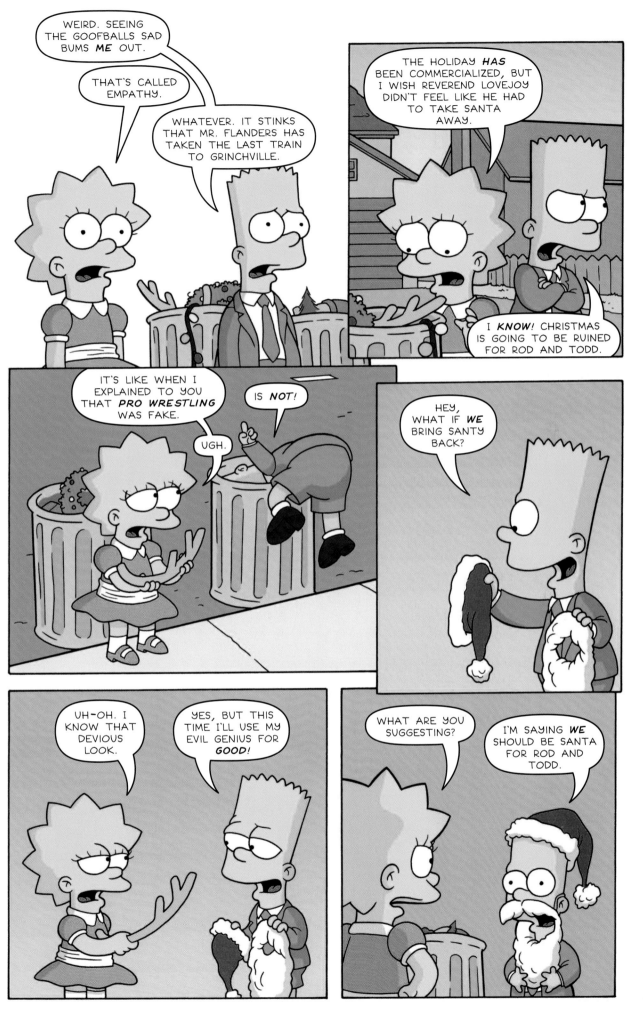

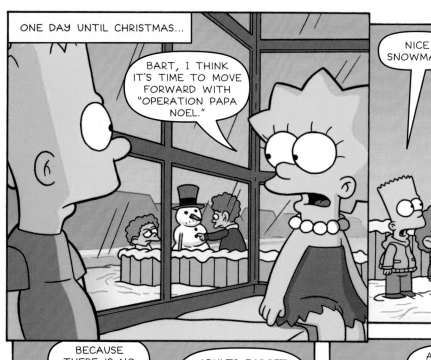

ONE DAY UNTIL CHRISTMAS...

BART, I THINK IT'S TIME TO MOVE FORWARD WITH "OPERATION PAPA NOEL."

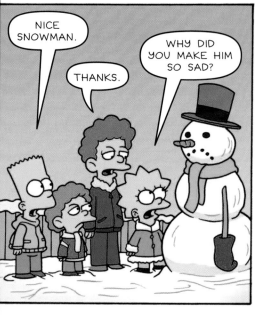

NICE SNOWMAN.

THANKS.

WHY DID YOU MAKE HIM SO SAD?

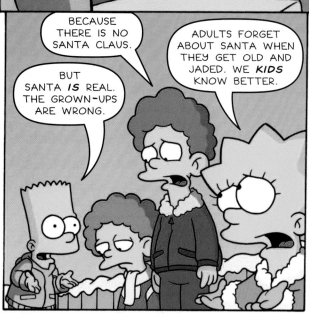

BECAUSE THERE IS NO SANTA CLAUS.

BUT SANTA *IS* REAL. THE GROWN-UPS ARE WRONG.

ADULTS FORGET ABOUT SANTA WHEN THEY GET OLD AND JADED. WE *KIDS* KNOW BETTER.

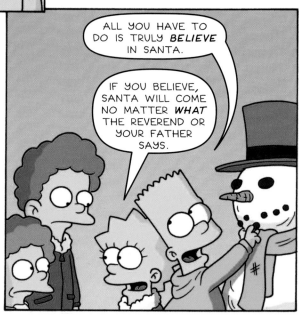

ALL YOU HAVE TO DO IS TRULY *BELIEVE* IN SANTA.

IF YOU BELIEVE, SANTA WILL COME NO MATTER *WHAT* THE REVEREND OR YOUR FATHER SAYS.

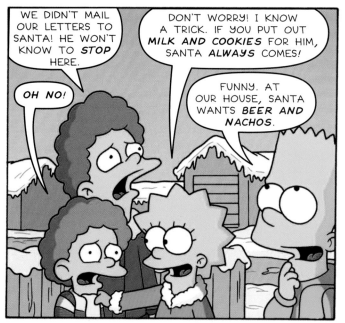

WE DIDN'T MAIL OUR LETTERS TO SANTA! HE WON'T KNOW TO *STOP* HERE.

OH NO!

DON'T WORRY! I KNOW A TRICK. IF YOU PUT OUT *MILK AND COOKIES* FOR HIM, SANTA *ALWAYS* COMES!

FUNNY. AT OUR HOUSE, SANTA WANTS *BEER AND NACHOS*.

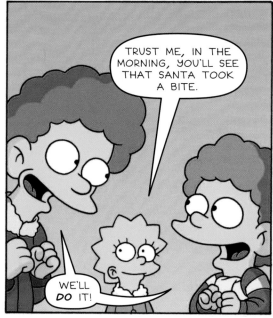

TRUST ME, IN THE MORNING, YOU'LL SEE THAT SANTA TOOK A BITE.

WE'LL *DO* IT!

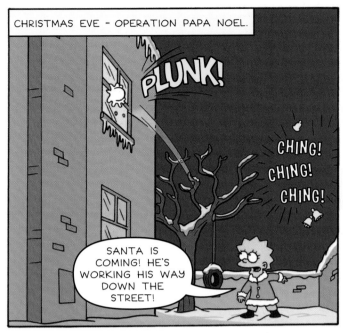

CHRISTMAS EVE - OPERATION PAPA NOEL.

PLUNK!

CHING! CHING! CHING!

SANTA IS COMING! HE'S WORKING HIS WAY DOWN THE STREET!

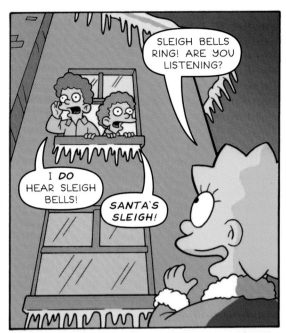

SLEIGH BELLS RING! ARE YOU LISTENING?

I *DO* HEAR SLEIGH BELLS!

SANTA'S SLEIGH!

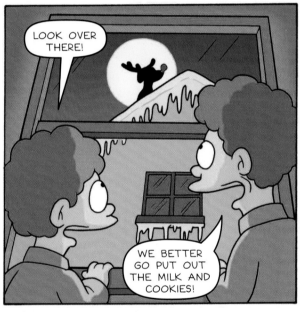

LOOK OVER THERE!

WE BETTER GO PUT OUT THE MILK AND COOKIES!

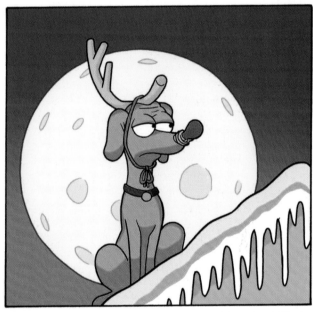

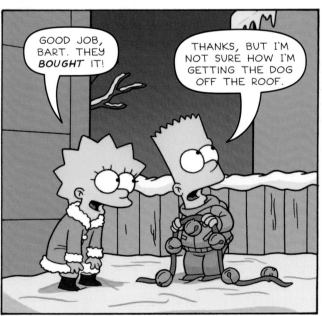

GOOD JOB, BART. THEY *BOUGHT* IT!

THANKS, BUT I'M NOT SURE HOW I'M GETTING THE DOG OFF THE ROOF.

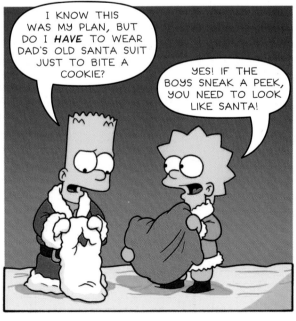

I KNOW THIS WAS MY PLAN, BUT DO I *HAVE* TO WEAR DAD'S OLD SANTA SUIT JUST TO BITE A COOKIE?

YES! IF THE BOYS SNEAK A PEEK, YOU NEED TO LOOK LIKE SANTA!

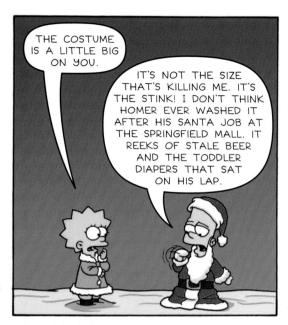

THE COSTUME IS A LITTLE BIG ON YOU.

IT'S NOT THE SIZE THAT'S KILLING ME. IT'S THE STINK! I DON'T THINK HOMER EVER WASHED IT AFTER HIS SANTA JOB AT THE SPRINGFIELD MALL. IT REEKS OF STALE BEER AND THE TODDLER DIAPERS THAT SAT ON HIS LAP.

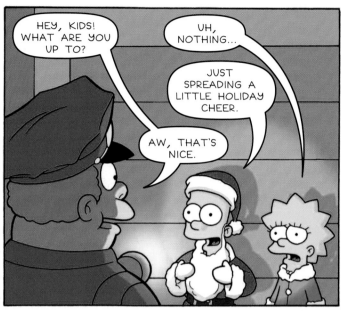

HEY, KIDS! WHAT ARE YOU UP TO?

UH, NOTHING...

JUST SPREADING A LITTLE HOLIDAY CHEER.

AW, THAT'S NICE.

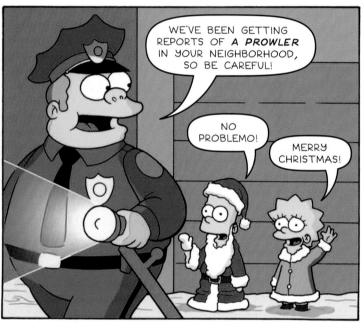

WE'VE BEEN GETTING REPORTS OF *A PROWLER* IN YOUR NEIGHBORHOOD, SO BE CAREFUL!

NO PROBLEMO!

MERRY CHRISTMAS!

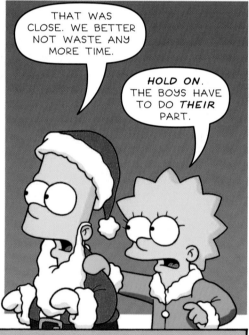

THAT WAS CLOSE. WE BETTER NOT WASTE ANY MORE TIME.

HOLD ON. THE BOYS HAVE TO DO *THEIR* PART.

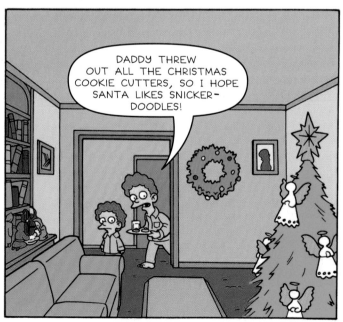

DADDY THREW OUT ALL THE CHRISTMAS COOKIE CUTTERS, SO I HOPE SANTA LIKES SNICKER-DOODLES!

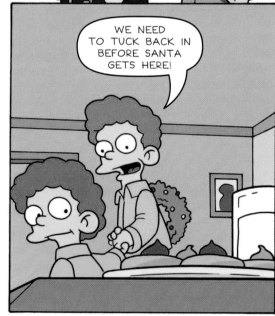

WE NEED TO TUCK BACK IN BEFORE SANTA GETS HERE!

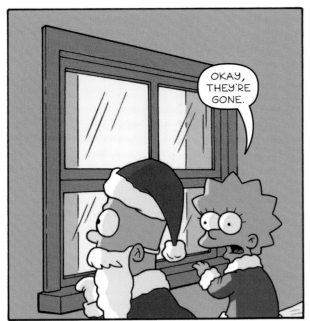

OKAY, THEY'RE GONE.

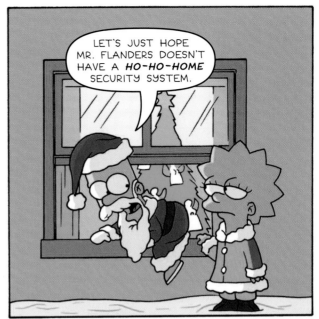

LET'S JUST HOPE MR. FLANDERS DOESN'T HAVE A *HO-HO-HOME* SECURITY SYSTEM.

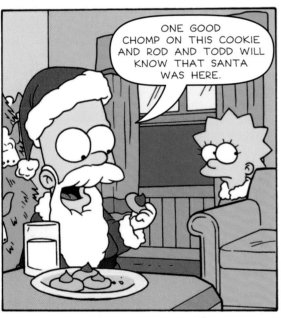

ONE GOOD CHOMP ON THIS COOKIE AND ROD AND TODD WILL KNOW THAT SANTA WAS HERE.

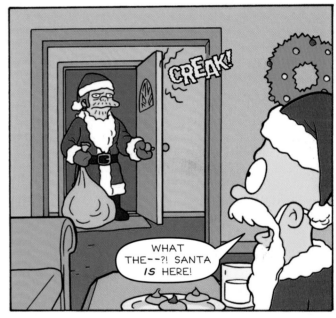

CREAK!

WHAT THE--?! SANTA *IS* HERE!

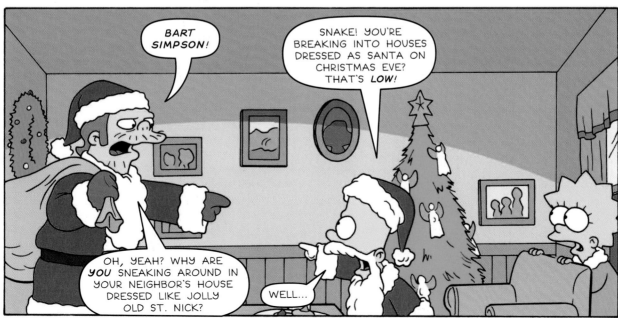

BART SIMPSON!

SNAKE! YOU'RE BREAKING INTO HOUSES DRESSED AS SANTA ON CHRISTMAS EVE? THAT'S *LOW!*

OH, YEAH? WHY ARE *YOU* SNEAKING AROUND IN YOUR NEIGHBOR'S HOUSE DRESSED LIKE JOLLY OLD ST. NICK?

WELL...

FREE-DIDDLY-EEZE THIEF-ARINO!
IS THAT A *FLARE GUN*?
A JUNIOR CAMPERS SCOUTMASTER SHOULD ALWAYS BE PREPARED! I'M PREPARED TO ***LIGHT YOU UP*** LIKE A CHRISTMAS TREE!
SANTA?
DADDY?
PLEASE DON'T SHOOT SANTA CLAUS!

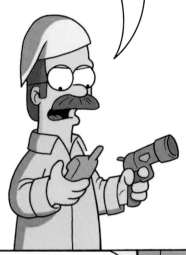

DADDY DOESN'T NEED TO POP A CA-DIDDLY-AP IN KRIS KRINGLE'S KEISTER. ONE CALL TO THE POLICE AND THEY'LL TAKE THIS *BAD SANTA* TO THE NORTH POLE PENITENTIARY.

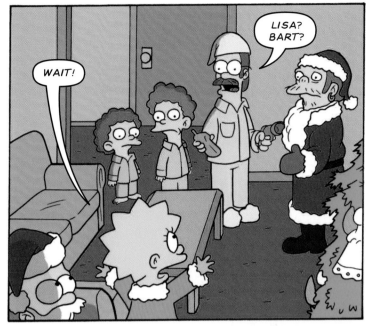

WAIT!

LISA? BART?

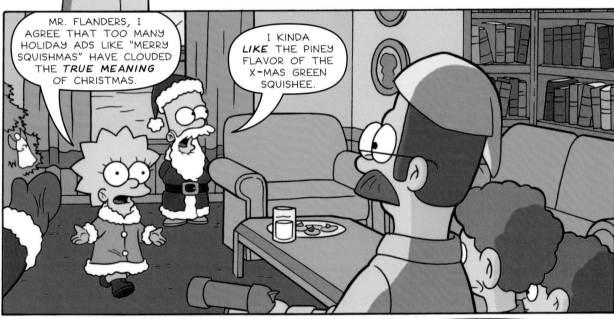

MR. FLANDERS, I AGREE THAT TOO MANY HOLIDAY ADS LIKE "MERRY SQUISHMAS" HAVE CLOUDED THE *TRUE MEANING* OF CHRISTMAS.

I KINDA *LIKE* THE PINEY FLAVOR OF THE X-MAS GREEN SQUISHEE.

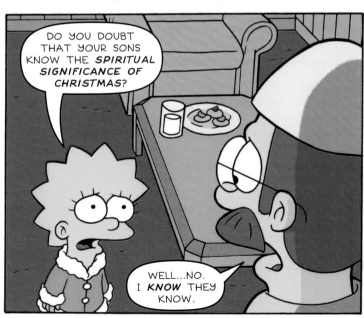

DO YOU DOUBT THAT YOUR SONS KNOW THE *SPIRITUAL SIGNIFICANCE OF CHRISTMAS?*

WELL...NO. I *KNOW* THEY KNOW.

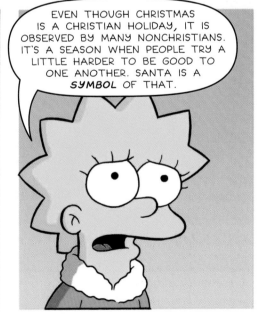

EVEN THOUGH CHRISTMAS IS A CHRISTIAN HOLIDAY, IT IS OBSERVED BY MANY NONCHRISTIANS. IT'S A SEASON WHEN PEOPLE TRY A LITTLE HARDER TO BE GOOD TO ONE ANOTHER. SANTA IS A *SYMBOL* OF THAT.

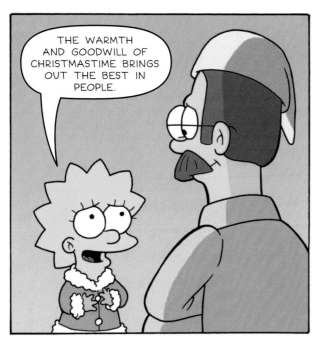

THE WARMTH AND GOODWILL OF CHRISTMASTIME BRINGS OUT THE BEST IN PEOPLE.

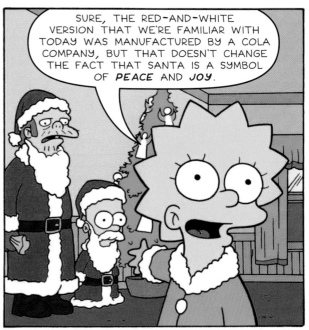

SURE, THE RED-AND-WHITE VERSION THAT WE'RE FAMILIAR WITH TODAY WAS MANUFACTURED BY A COLA COMPANY, BUT THAT DOESN'T CHANGE THE FACT THAT SANTA IS A SYMBOL OF *PEACE* AND *JOY*.

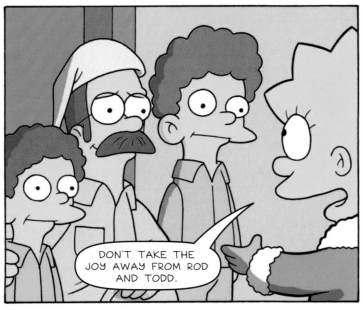

DON'T TAKE THE JOY AWAY FROM ROD AND TODD.

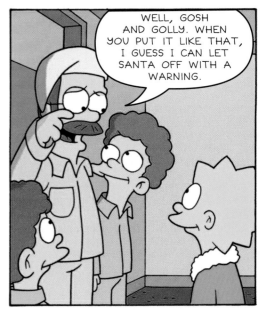

WELL, GOSH AND GOLLY. WHEN YOU PUT IT LIKE THAT, I GUESS I CAN LET SANTA OFF WITH A WARNING.

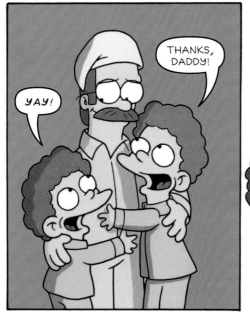

YAY!

THANKS, DADDY!

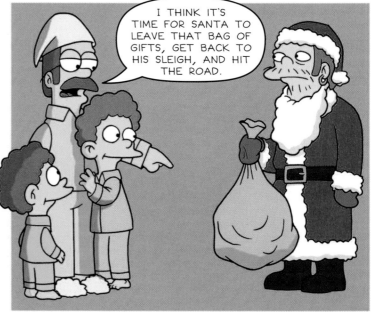

I THINK IT'S TIME FOR SANTA TO LEAVE THAT BAG OF GIFTS, GET BACK TO HIS SLEIGH, AND HIT THE ROAD.

HERE, LITTLE DUDES.
MERRY CHRISTMAS TO ALL, AND TO ALL A GOOD NIGHT!
MALIBU STACY
A MALIBU STACY SCIENTIFIC CALCULATOR!
WHAT IS **THIS**?
THAT'S A VIDEO GAME BUT YOU CAN'T PLAY IT WITHOUT AN X-STATION.
I STILL LIKE IT. IT'S SHINY!
GRAND THEFT SKATEBOARD
AW, MAN! SNAKE HIT **OUR** HOUSE BEFORE HE CAME HERE. THOSE WERE **OUR** GIFTS!
TO: Bart
LISA, YOU WERE RIGHT. REVEREND LOVEJOY AND I WENT A SMIDGE OVERBOARD. THANK YOU FOR REMINDING ME OF THE ***SIMPLE JOYS*** OF CHRISTMAS.
YEAH, SOMETIMES IT IS BETTER TO GIVE THAN RECEIVE.
YOU'RE WELCOME.
HEY, SOMEONE STOLE MY SIX-PACK OF JINGLE BREW! ***CHRISTMAS IS RUINED!***
THE END

CHRISTMAS EVE at

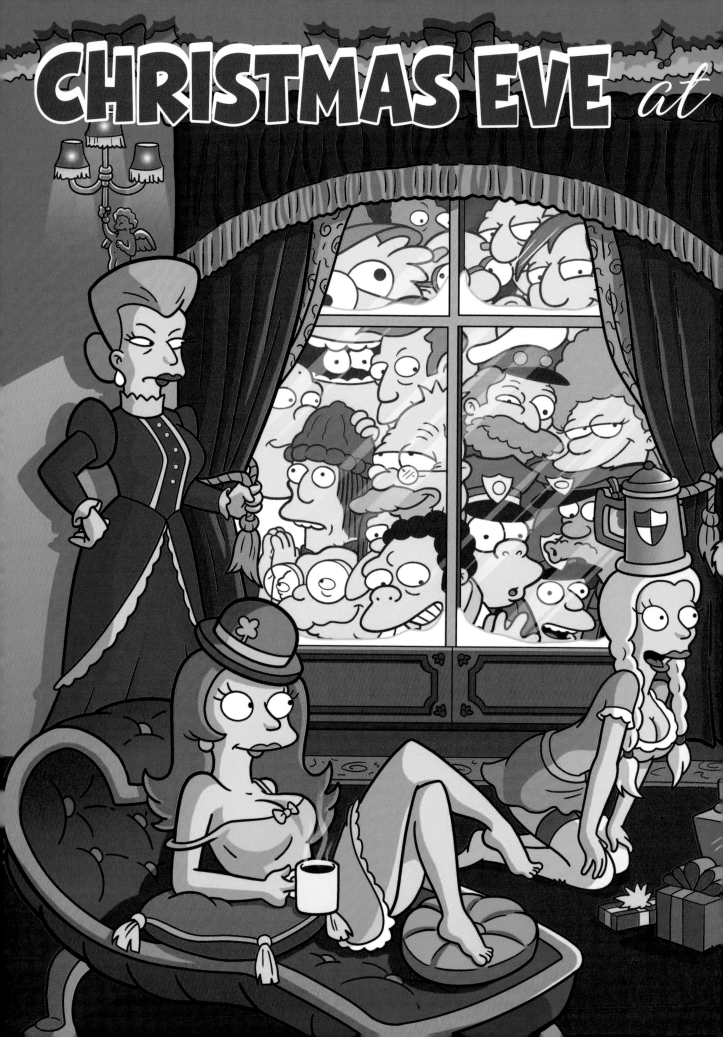

MAISON DERRIÈRE
Belle
Gigi
Candy
Dixie

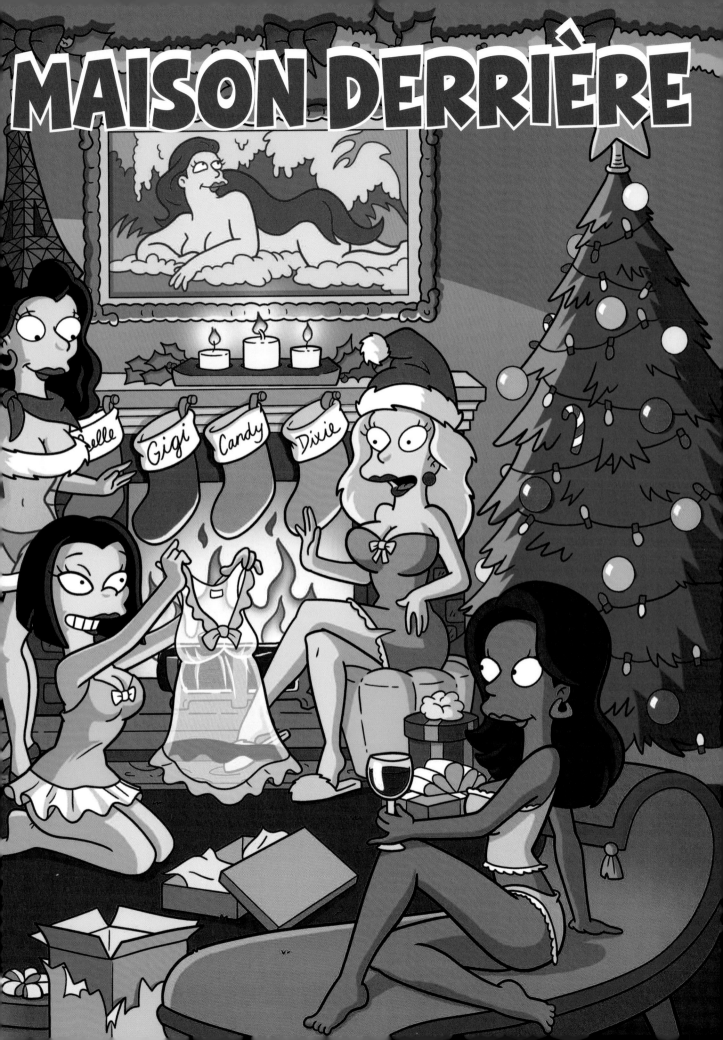

Why wait for summer? Wintertime is fun time at

BOBSLED DOWN THE SPLATTERHORN!
SLASH MOUNTAIN
TORTURE LAND
MAKE A NEW FRIEND AT SANTA ITCHY'S PETTING ZOO!
MR. ITCHY'S INEBRIATED RIDE
UNNECESSARY SURGERY LAND
WIN FIRST PRIZE AT SCRATCHY'S ICE SCULPTURE CONTEST!
THE MAI
THE PEOPLE SMOOSHER

Itchy & Scratchy's Holiday Wonderland!

HOMER'S NEW YEAR'S RESOLUTIONS

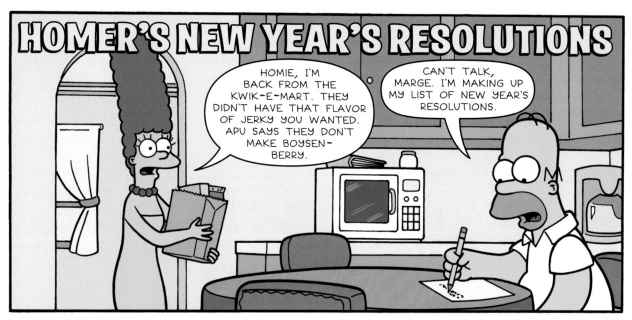

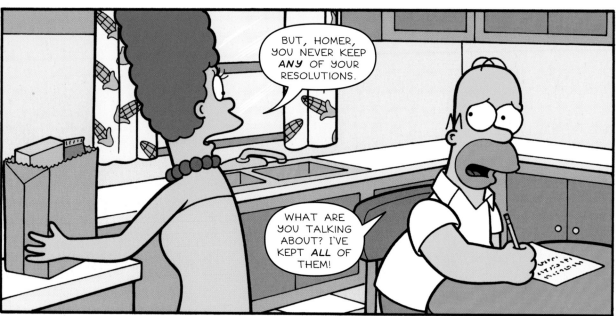

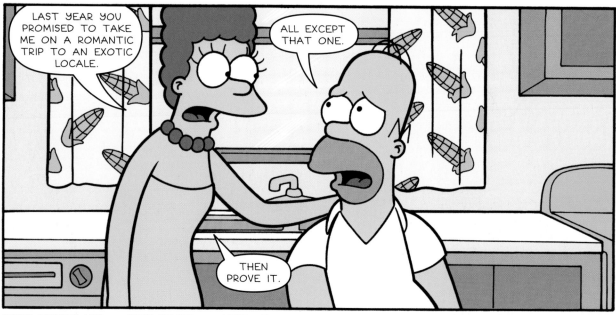

TONY DIGEROLAMO
SCRIPT

JOEY NILGES
PENCILS

MIKE DECARLO
INKS

ART VILLANUEVA
COLORS

KAREN BATES
LETTERS

BILL MORRISON
EDITOR

"REMEMBER WHEN I VOWED THAT I WOULD LOSE WEIGHT?"
LOOK, MARGE! I LOST TWO POUNDS!
YOU DIDN'T LOSE ANY WEIGHT. YOU JUST REPLACED YOUR REGULAR CLOTHES WITH CLOTHES MADE OUT OF PAPER.
"HOW ABOUT WHEN I RESOLVED TO PUT A BRAND NEW BLADE ON FLANDERS' LAWN MOWER? BOY! THAT WORKED GREAT!"
Property of Ned Flanders
WELL, I GUESS THAT WAS NICE. DID YOU RETURN THE LAWN MOWER?
YEAH, YEAH, YEAH...I'LL GET TO IT. THE POINT IS I MOWED THE LAWN.
WE WERE TALKING ABOUT YOUR RESOLUTIONS.
BUT I'M TELLING YOU, I KEEP THEM, MARGE!
"I PROMISED I'D SPEND MORE TIME WITH THE KIDS."
SUCK SUCK
"AND I PROMISED I'D DRINK FEWER MUGS OF BEER."
I GOTTA RETHINK THIS DRINK SPECIAL.

OH, HOMIE, ALL OF A SUDDEN I DON'T FEEL SO GOOD. I THINK THAT CHICKEN SALAD I ATE EARLIER ISN'T SITTING WELL.
⁝GASP!⁝ YOU ATE MY CHICKEN SALAD?! BUT I WAS GOING TO EAT THAT WHEN I FINISHED MY LIST!
DID YOU COOK THE CHICKEN ALL THE WAY THROUGH?
OH, MARGE, DON'T BE SILLY. YOU DON'T **COOK** SALADS.
I THINK YOU'D BETTER TAKE ME TO THE HOSPITAL. I'M GOING... TO...
DON'T WORRY, MARGE, I'LL TAKE CARE OF EVERY-THING!

THE NEXT DAY IN A HOSPITAL IN JAMAICA...
THIS IS NOT WHAT I MEANT BY A ROMANTIC TRIP TO AN EXOTIC LOCALE.
THESE ARE MY NEW YEAR'S RESOLUTIONS, MARGE. I GET TO DECIDE HOW TO KEEP THEM!
PIÑA COLADA I.V., HONEY?
THE END

from KING TOOT'S Holiday Album Bargain Bin!

THE BE SHARPS
BIGGER THAN BABY JESUS!!
THIS SPECIAL FAN-CLUB-ONLY RELEASE INCLUDES THE TIMELESS HITS:
SANTA BABY ONBOARD
I'LL BE (SHARP) HOME FOR CHRISTMAS
AND HARK! THE HERALD ANGELS HEAR US SING (AND LOVE US)!
PARTY POSSE
X-MAS X-TREME
FEATURING:
WE NEED A LITTLE X-BOX
I SAW MOMMY KISSING SIDESHOW BOB
CHRISTMAS IN JUVIE
KRUSTY
KLOWNS KLEZMER!
Featuring:
The Dreidel Song
The Other Dreidel Song

CLETUS SPUCKLER'S
JUG BAND KRISMUS
FEATURING:
GRANDMA GOT RUN OVER BY A JOHN DEERE
WHOSE KID IS THIS?
ALL I WANT FOR CHRISTMAS IS SOME NEW FRONT TEETH
SONGS INCLUDE:
FROSTY, THE COLD BEER
OH COME, ALL YE BOOZEHOUNDS
THE TWELVE DUFFS OF CHRISTMAS
Happy Holiduff!
SEASON'S CHUGGINGS FROM YOUR FRIENDS AT DUFF
DUFF
D
NUCLEAR WINTER WONDERLAND
NOW AVAILABLE ON
EDISON WAX CYLINDER™
AND PLAYER PIANO ROLL!
BY
"CHRISTMAS"
MONTGOMERY BURNS

RALPH VS. WILD

Junior Camper SNOW SLED Jamboree

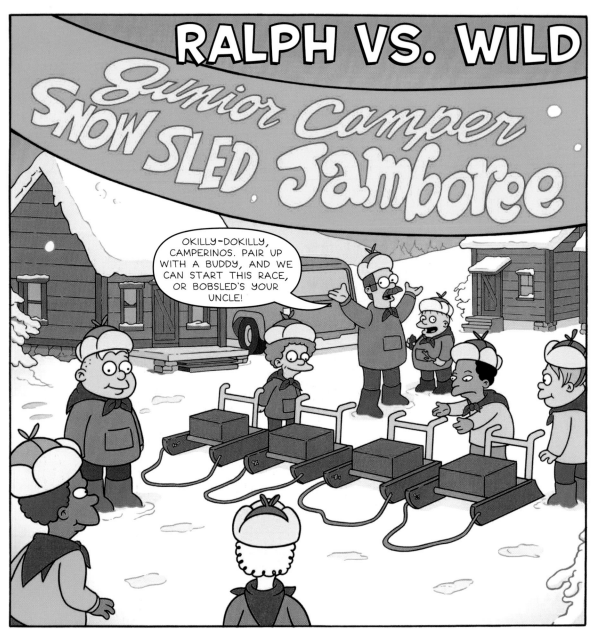

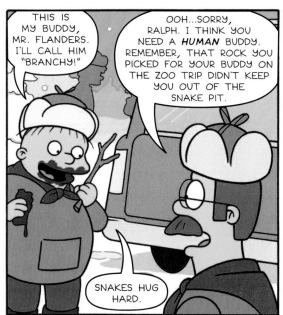

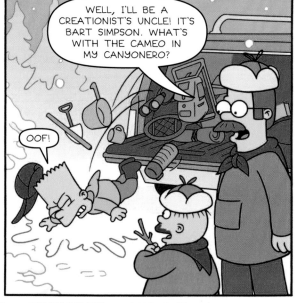

TONY DIGEROLAMO
SCRIPT

JOHN COSTANZA
PENCILS

PHYLLIS NOVIN
INKS

ROBERT STANLEY
COLORS

KAREN BATES
LETTERS

BILL MORRISON
EDITOR

UH...SORRY FOR HIDING IN YOUR CAR. I MADE BEER ICICLES WITH HOMER'S LAST SIX-PACK, SO I'M KIND OF LYING LOW UNTIL HIS RAGE DIES DOWN. WHERE AM I?
AT THE JUNIOR CAMPER SNOW SLED JAMBOREE! AND YOU'RE JUST IN TIME TO BE RALPH'S SLED BUDDY!
YOU MEAN AS IN SLED VIDEO GAME TOURNAMENT, RIGHT?
WELL, IF YOU CLOSE YOUR EYES AND PICTURE A TOBOGGAN IN YOUR NOGGIN', YOU CAN *PRETEND* IT'S A VIDEO GAME!
YAY! BART'S MY BUDDY!
GROAN!
MINUTES LATER...
ON YOUR MAR-DIDDILY-ARKS!
CAN I RIDE THE SLED, TOO?
I'LL RIDE FOR BOTH OF US.
YAY!
GET SET! GO-DIDDILY-*O*!
WHOA! GO, RALPH! HEY, WE MIGHT ACTUALLY WIN THIS THING.
WEEEEE! I'M *MUSHING*!
NO, RALPH! YOU'RE MUSHING *THE WRONG WAY*!
AH, HA, HAHA, AH, HA, HAHA! BUNNY!

TEN MINUTES LATER...
I'M HELP-DING.
WELL, YOU'D BETTER START "HELP-DING" ME FIND THIS GIANT "N" THAT'S ON THE MAP!
N
W S E
TWO HOURS LATER...
OKAY, IF I CAN JUST GET THIS FIRE GOING, WE WON'T FREEZE TO DEATH. AND THEN MAYBE WE CAN SEND SMOKE SIGNALS. YOU SPEAK SMOKE, RIGHT?
SCRATCH
SCRATCH
SCRATCH
I DID IT! I GOT THE FIRE STARTED! I'M NOT GOING TO DIE! HA-HA! TAKE THAT, *HOMER'S BOOK OF PROPHECY*!
HOMER'S BOOK OF PROFECY
FIRE'S BAD.
MY DADDY SAYS, "NO MORE FIRES IN THE HOUSE."
AHHHHH!
FWUMP!
MINUTES LATER...
OKAY, ACCORDING TO THE *JUNIOR CAMPERS SURVIVAL GUIDE*, I CAN USE A MIRROR TO SIGNAL A PASSING PLANE.
YECCH...THIS MIRROR'S COVERED IN CHOCOLATE!
IT'S SHINY. LIKE MY CELL PHONE.

I'M FREEZING MY BUTT OFF OUT HERE, AND YOU HAD A CELL PHONE THE WHOLE TIME?!
WHEN IT RUMBLES, IT MAKES ME ALL TICKLY.
IT'S NOT CHARGED. DON'T YOU KNOW HOW TO CHARGE A PHONE?
I'M NOT ALLOWED TO USE THE 'LEC-TRICK-SKITY.
WE'RE DOOMED.
RALPH, JUST PROMISE ME THAT WHEN I DIE HERE IN THE SNOW, YOU'LL MAKE SURE MY FACE FREEZES IN A HILARIOUS EXPRESSION.
I WANT TO REALLY FREAK OUT LISA AT MY FUNERAL.
OKAY!
BOYS!
BARK! BARK!
I WAS SO WORRIED.
AW, MAN. I THOUGHT WE WERE GONERS! HOW'D YOU FIND US?
ACTUALLY IT WAS ALL DUE TO RALPH...
HE HUGGED SO MANY THINGS IN THE WOODS, HE LEFT A TRAIL OF CHOCOLATE HAND PRINTS FOR US TO FOLLOW.
NICE GOING, RALPH. YOU'VE JUST EARNED A SURVIVAL MERIT BADGE!
D'OH!
YAY! I SURVIVE-DED!
THE END

HAPPY HANUKKAH
Hanukkah at
SCHTICKFAIR

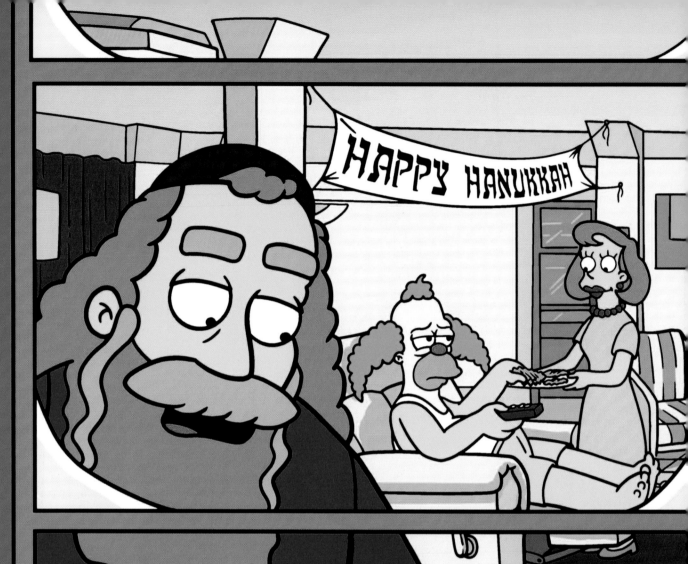

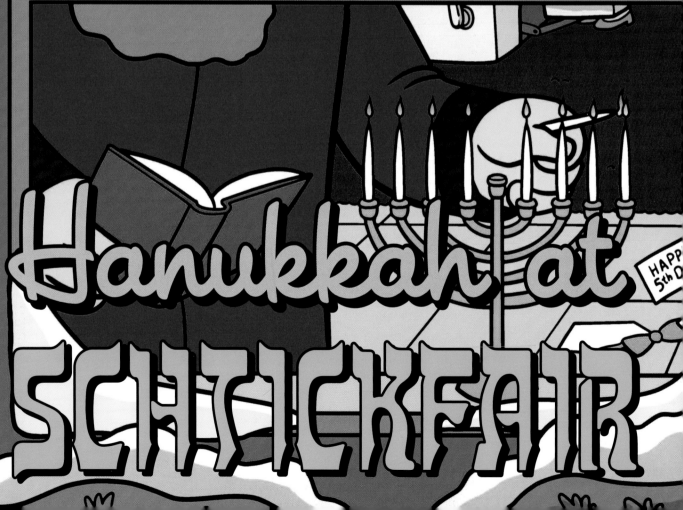

HAPPY 7th DAY!
HAPPY 8th DAY!
HAPPY 4th DAY!
HAPPY DAY!

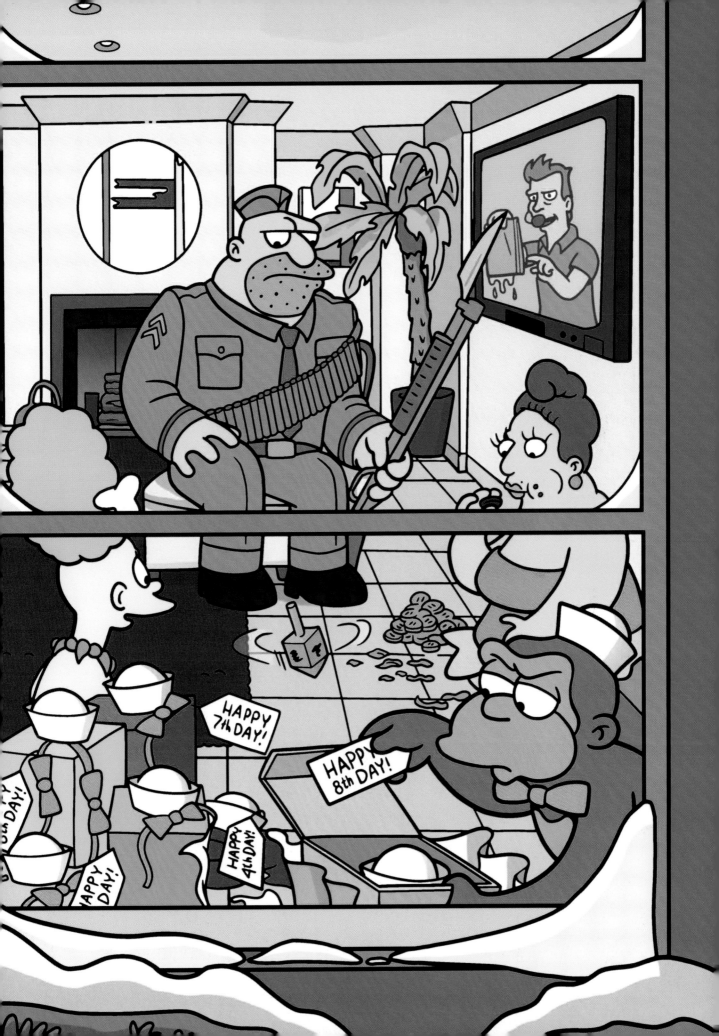

TIME'S A-WASTIN', MAN!
HOMER'S LAST-MINUTE GIFT LIST
MARGE - Evening out doing what marge likes (find out what marge likes!)
BART - Get-out-of-whupping-free card (ask Lisa to design!)
LISA - Some smarty-pants book (more research needed here!!!)
MAGGIE - Half rattle/half pacifier... Rattle-Cifier!! (must build!!)
SANTA'S LITTLE HELPER - More playtime with cat (see below!!!)
SNOWBALL II (or possibly V) - more playtime with dog (see above!!!)
DAD - Gift T.B.D. (find out what T.B.D. stands for!!!!!)
PATTY & SELMA - (d'oh! Running out of time... Christmas morning...hags at the door! Need alibi...hide in garage until January...
TOO LATE!!!!!!)

HOMER, THE CHILDREN ARE UP WAY PAST THEIR BEDTIME.
DON'T WORRY, MARGE, THEY HAVE ALL YEAR TO CATCH UP ON THEIR SLEEP.
...AND HERE'S HOPING WE ALL MAKE A TRIED AND TRUE EFFORT TO **KEEP** OUR RESOLUTIONS IN THE **NEW YEAR**...
BUT FIRST, LET'S REMEMBER THE RESOLUTIONS THAT WE **COULDN'T** KEEP SO WE CAN AVOID MAKING THE SAME MISTAKES.
BART, WE'LL BEGIN WITH YOUR RESOLUTION TO NEVER MAKE NOISES USING MORE THAN ONE ORIFICE AT A TI--
OOMPH!
HAPPY NEW YEAR AND WELCOME TO PLANET HYPE, THE WORLD'S LARGEST **CELEBRITY-THEMED** CHAIN RESTAURANT. THIS IS THE CLOSEST MOST OF YOU WILL EVER COME TO HOLLYWOOD IN YOUR FLABBY LITTLE LIVES.
PLANET HYPE
OH, IT'S JUST ABOUT **MIDNIGHT!** GET READY FOR THE COUNTDOWN.
NO ONE THROW AWAY ANYTHING HE TOUCHES! BY THE TIME I'M DONE POSTING THIS JUNK ON **EBUY**, THIS DINNER WILL HAVE PAID FOR ITSELF!
IT'S GOING TO BE A HAPPY NEW YEAR INDEED FOR **YOURS TRULY**, IF MY **RESOLUTION KEEPER 3000** WORKS AS PLANNED...
NOW I'LL JUST POSITION MYSELF IN THE MIDDLE OF THE RESTAURANT LIKE SO, THEN MAKE WITH THE TURNING ON OF THE MACHINE AND THE WAITING FOR THE **MAGIC** TO HAPPEN...
CLICK!

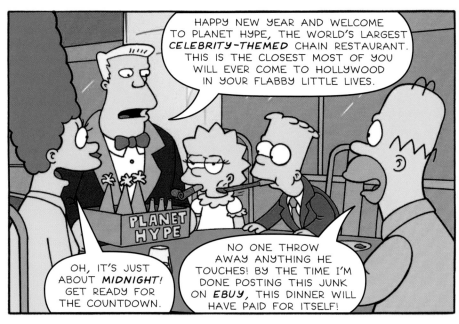

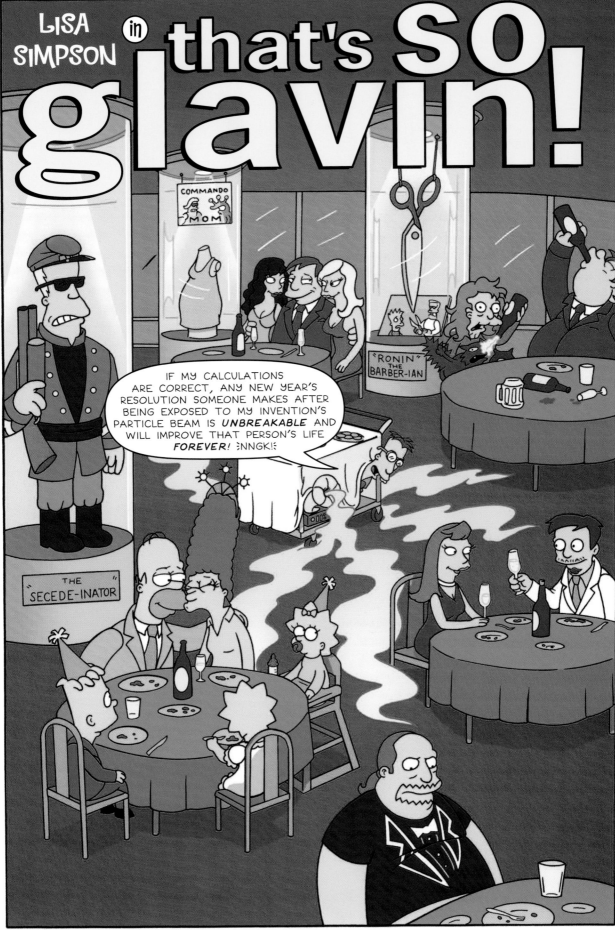

LISA SIMPSON in that's SO glavin!

IF MY CALCULATIONS ARE CORRECT, ANY NEW YEAR'S RESOLUTION SOMEONE MAKES AFTER BEING EXPOSED TO MY INVENTION'S PARTICLE BEAM IS *UNBREAKABLE* AND WILL IMPROVE THAT PERSON'S LIFE *FOREVER!* ∋NNGK!∈

COMMANDO MOM

"RONIN" THE BARBER-IAN

"THE SECEDE-INATOR"

ERIC ROGERS
SCRIPT

JOEY NILGES
PENCILS

KEN WHEATON
INKS

ROBERT STANLEY
COLORS

KAREN BATES
LETTERS

BILL MORRISON
EDITOR

I KNOW I SAY IT EVERY YEAR, BUT THIS TIME I MEAN IT! I AM GOING TO LOSE WEIGHT AND KEEP IT OFF!
NO MORE! I AM GOING TO STOP DATING THESE HOT, NUBILE BIMBOS AND...ER, AH...RE-DEDICATE MYSELF TO MY FAITHFUL WIFE.
BRRRING!
THE WIFE
PERHAPS IF I AM A TAD MORE FRIENDLY AND LESS CRITICAL TO ONE AND ALL, I WON'T FIND MYSELF SO VERY ALONE NEXT NEW YEAR'S EVE.
YOU KNOW, SWEETIE, I THINK YOU'RE RIGHT ...I WOULD BE A MUCH BETTER DOCTOR IF I ACTUALLY WENT TO A LEGITIMATE MEDICAL SCHOOL. I'M GOING TO ENROLL FIRST THING TOMORROW!
EERRAAAHBLABBABABA GRRAWW...CATS!
I COULDN'T AGREE MORE... PERHAPS WE ALL SHOULD GIVE MORE. I'M GOING TO TRY AND BE JUST LIKE YOU THIS YEAR, AND I'LL START BY PAYING OFF MY TAB AT MOE'S.
NOW I SHALL TRACK MY NEW LITTLE GUINEA PIGS OVER THE COURSE OF THE YEAR HEY LADY! AND DOCUMENT MY FINDINGS, WHICH WILL UNDOUBTEDLY LEAD TO MY WINNING OF THE NOBEL PRIZE!

THE NEXT DAY...
HOMIE, YOU'RE GOING TO NEED THIS IF YOU'RE GOING TO SHOVEL SNOW OFF THE DRIVEWAY, AREN'T YOU?
NO TIME, MARGE! I'M GOING OUT FOR A RUN. EVERYTHING ELSE CAN WAIT UNTIL I START TO SHED THESE EXCESS POUNDS!
GO, HOME-BOY!
ALL RIGHT, DAD!
JOE! WHAT'S ALL THIS ABOUT?
BREAKFAST IN BED, HONEY. I'VE DECIDED THAT I'M GOING TO BE A BETTER...ER, AH... HUSBAND TO YOU THIS YEAR, STARTING NOW!
HARK, FAIR MAIDEN! LET ME SHIELD YOU FROM WINTER'S SLUSHY KISS WITH MY AUTHENTIC "FALL GUY" LEATHER JACKET!
OH MY, WHAT A GENTLE-MAN!
THE FALL GUY
SEASON 3
83 - 84
SO IS IT VERY HARD TO GET INTO THIS MEDICAL SCHOOL?
DO YOU LIKE DISSECTING LIVING THINGS AND SAYING THE WORD "STAT?"
WHO DOESN'T?
THEN YOU'RE IN!
SMC
SPRINGFIELD MEDICAL COLLEGE
ADMITTED
HAPPY NEW YEAR, MOE. HERE'S FIVE DOLLARS TO GO TOWARD PAYING OFF MY TAB.
HA HA HA! GOOD ONE, BARN. HERE, FIRST DRINK OF THE YEAR'S ON ME!
NO WAY! I WON'T TAKE ANOTHER DRINK FROM YOU UNLESS I'VE PAID FOR IT, AND I CAN'T DO THAT UNTIL I'VE PAID OFF MY ENTIRE TAB! SO GOOD DAY TO YOU, SIR!

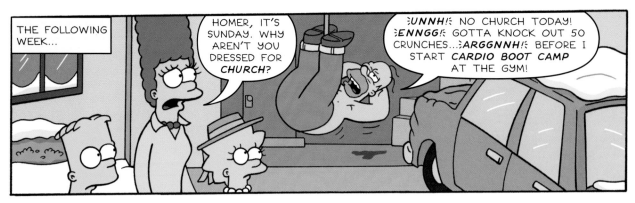

THE FOLLOWING WEEK...

HOMER, IT'S SUNDAY. WHY AREN'T YOU DRESSED FOR *CHURCH*?

〔UNNH!〕 NO CHURCH TODAY! 〔ENNGG!〕 GOTTA KNOCK OUT 50 CRUNCHES...〔ARGGNNH!〕 BEFORE I START *CARDIO BOOT CAMP* AT THE GYM!

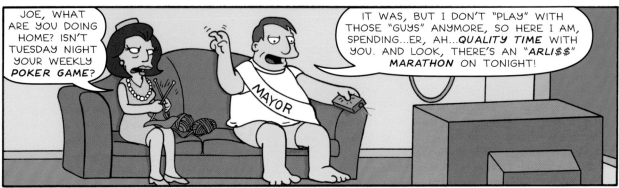

JOE, WHAT ARE YOU DOING HOME? ISN'T TUESDAY NIGHT YOUR WEEKLY *POKER GAME*?

IT WAS, BUT I DON'T "PLAY" WITH THOSE "GUYS" ANYMORE, SO HERE I AM, SPENDING...ER, AH...*QUALITY TIME* WITH YOU. AND LOOK, THERE'S AN *"ARLI$$"* *MARATHON* ON TONIGHT!

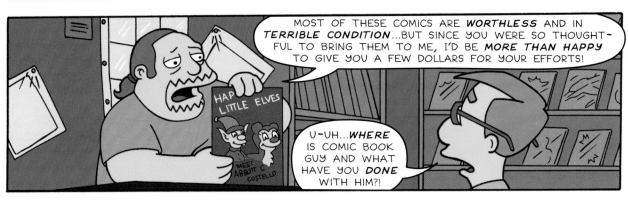

MOST OF THESE COMICS ARE *WORTHLESS* AND IN *TERRIBLE CONDITION*...BUT SINCE YOU WERE SO THOUGHT-FUL TO BRING THEM TO ME, I'D BE *MORE THAN HAPPY* TO GIVE YOU A FEW DOLLARS FOR YOUR EFFORTS!

HAP LITTLE ELVES

MEET ABBOTT & COSTELLO

U-UH...*WHERE* IS COMIC BOOK GUY AND WHAT HAVE YOU *DONE* WITH HIM?!

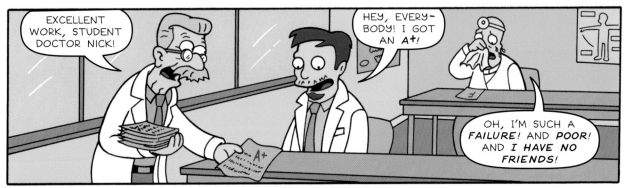

EXCELLENT WORK, STUDENT DOCTOR NICK!

HEY, EVERY-BODY! I GOT AN A⁺!

A⁺

OH, I'M SUCH A *FAILURE*! AND *POOR*! AND *I HAVE NO FRIENDS*!

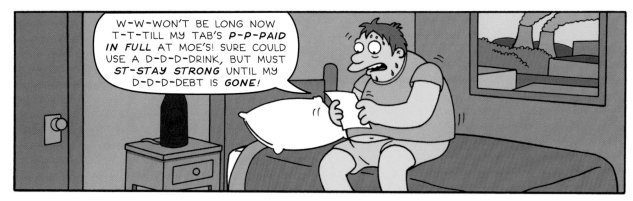

W-W-WON'T BE LONG NOW T-T-TILL MY TAB'S *P-P-PAID IN FULL* AT MOE'S! SURE COULD USE A D-D-D-DRINK, BUT MUST *ST-STAY STRONG* UNTIL MY D-D-D-DEBT IS *GONE*!

KRUSTY'S RACE FOR THE CURE
WAY TO GO, HOMIE!
LOOKIN' GOOD, HOMER!
I'M SWEATIN' JUST WATCHIN' YOU!
YES! I'M THE BEST! THIS IS THE GREATEST DAY OF MY LIFE!
0802
HEY HEY! WE HAVE A WINNER! AND TO PRESENT THE TROPHY, HERE'S THE CURE'S LEAD SINGER...ROBERT SMITH.
AW, CRIPES! IF I'D KNOWN HOMER HAD A CHANCE IN HELL AT WINNING THIS THING, I WOULDN'T HAVE PUT FIVE BENJIES ON THE ETHIOPIAN!
WHERE ARE YOU GOING, SWEETHEART? I THOUGHT WE WERE GOING TO...ER, AH...SPEND THE AFTERNOON ORGANIZING MY SASHES BY COLOR AND ELECTORIAL TERM!
SORRY, JOE, I CAN'T... I FORGOT THAT I HAVE A THING WITH...UH...YOU KNOW WHO AT... ERMM...THAT ONE PLACE. YOU GO AHEAD. I'LL BE HOME LATE, DON'T WAIT UP FOR ME!
AYE, CARUMBA! WHAT THE HECK HAPPENED IN HERE?
COMIC BOOK GUY IS SO NICE THAT HE CAN'T SAY NO TO ANYONE WHO WANTS TO SELL HIM THEIR COMICS, TOYS, OR ANYTHING ELSE!
...DON'T WORRY THAT YOU PUT BOOGERS ON THE KNIVES OF YOUR "STAB 'EM, JAB 'EM JAILBOTS" TOY. I'LL BE HAPPY TO REMOVE THEM MYSELF.
507
JAILBOTS LIKE TO SHIV MY NOSE!
...FURTHERMORE, DEAN, THIS STUDENT HAS SCORED PERFECTLY ON EVERY EXAM, AND I FEEL THAT WE SHOULD ACCELERATE HIS CURRICULUM.
IF HE CONTINUES IN THIS MANNER, HE WILL BECOME THE FIRST STUDENT IN MEDICAL SCHOOL HISTORY TO GRADUATE IN SIX MONTHS' TIME!
DONE!
DEAN
SO YOU'RE SAYING I'M ACTUALLY A MEDICAL GENIUS? WOW! WHO KNEW?
THAT'S THE LAST OF THE MONEY YOU OWE, BARNEY...YOU DID IT! YOU PAID OFF YOUR ENTIRE TAB!
AND I'M COMPLETELY SOBER, TOO!
I GUESS I'VE GOT TO FIND SOMETHING TO DO WITH ALL THIS EXTRA MONEY AND ENERGY--
GOT TOO MUCH EXTRA MONEY AND ENERGY? WHY NOT GIVE IT BACK TO THE UNIVERSE FROM WHICH YOU WERE CREATED? JOIN US AT THE CHURCH OF SCIENTRICKERY, JUST OFF ROUTE 4 NEAR LARD LAD'S...

SIX MONTHS LATER...
KENT BROCKMAN "LIVE" ON THE SCENE TO PRESENT THIS YEAR'S "FITTEST MAN IN SPRINGFIELD" AWARD TO NONE OTHER THAN HOMER J. SIMPSON!
AN OUTSTANDING HONOR I HAVE WON THIRTEEN TIMES MYSELF, HOMER.
IN LIGHT OF YOUR TREMENDOUS ACHIEVEMENTS, I AM OFFERING YOU THE FULL-TIME JOB OF BEING MY PERSONAL TRAINER.
FITNESS MONTHLY
WOO-HOO! YOUR OPTIMUM FITNESS WILL COME BEFORE NOTHING ELSE IN MY LIFE!
DIVORCE PAPERS?! YOU CAN'T LEAVE ME IN THE MIDDLE OF AN ELECTION! THE PEOPLE OF SPRINGFIELD WON'T ELECT SOMEONE WHO'S A FAILURE IN HIS PERSONAL LIFE! I NEED YOU!
QUIMBY!
I'M SORRY, JOE, BUT AFTER SPENDING SO MUCH TIME WITH YOU THESE PAST FEW MONTHS, I REALIZE THAT I JUST DON'T LOVE YOU ANYMORE.
MAYOR
VOTE QUIMBY
HEAVENS TO MURGATROID...MY GLORIOUS SHOP! WHO DID THIS?
THE BLAZE STARTED BECAUSE OF A FAULTY ELECTRICAL OUTLET,
BUT THE FIRE COULD HAVE BEEN PREVENTED IF THERE WASN'T SO MUCH FLAMMABLE STUFF IN THE SHOP.
HI, EVERYBODY...WELCOME TO MY NEW CLINIC! I OFFER THE LOWEST PRICES FOR THE QUICKEST RESULTS IN ALL OF SPRINGFIELD!
PLUS, I HAVE AN ACTUAL MEDICAL DEGREE NOW, SO EVERYTHING I DO ISN'T JUST A GUESS ANYMORE!
AND NOW THAT YOU HAVE GIVEN YOUR WEEKLY EARNINGS TO THE CHURCH, IT IS TIME TO OFFER SACRIFICE TO THE GODDESS BARBARELLA IN THE FORM OF THIS PHILLY CHEESE STEAK WITH EXTRA ONIONS, JUST THE WAY SHE LIKES IT.
♫ EXTRA ONIONS... ♫

DECEMBER 31ST...
...I'M SORRY, MARGE, BUT RAINIER'S NEW MOVIE STARTS SHOOTING MONDAY IN A REMOTE AREA OF ANTARCTICA AND I HAVE TO FLY OUT FIRST THING IN THE MORNING.
BUT IT'S NEW YEAR'S EVE, HOMER...WHAT ABOUT THE KIDS? WHAT ABOUT ME? WHO'S GOING TO TAKE CARE OF US?
YOU'LL BE FINE. I'LL ONLY BE GONE FOR EIGHT MONTHS. AND WITH ALL YOUR FREE TIME, MAYBE YOU CAN GET IN SHAPE, TOO.
CONGRATULATION
MAYOR
MY FELLOW SPRINGFIELDIANS, I THANK YOU FOR YOUR CONFIDENCE IN ME AND PROMISE TO LEAD OUR FAIR CITY TO NEW HEIGHTS.
FOR MY FIRST OFFICIAL ACT AS MAYOR, I WILL DO AWAY WITH THE MAYORAL SASH AND REPLACE IT WITH A FINE SATIN ASCOT!
UNEMPLO
HAW HAW!
WILL WORK 4 COMICS
HI-DIDDILY-HO, KIND VAGRANT! THOUGHT YOU MIGHT LIKE THESE USED COPIES OF MY BOYS' GRAPHIC NOVEL, "300...WAYS TO SPREAD THE GOSPEL!"
I'M SORRY, APU, BUT I CAN'T SEE YOUR CHILDREN ANYMORE. MY OFFICES ARE CLOSED FOR GOOD AS OF TODAY, SO I SUGGEST YOU GO SEE DR. NICK.
FOR LEASE!
BUT HIS CLINIC IS TOO BUSY FROM HAVING PUT EVERY OTHER DOCTOR IN SPRINGFIELD OUT OF BUSINESS! MY CHILDREN WILL NOT BE GETTING IN FOR EXAMINATION FOR AT LEAST TWO MONTHS!
...SO YOU'RE SURE YOU DON'T WANT TO COME PARTY WITH US? IT'S NEW YEAR'S EVE, BARN!
I'M SORRY, BUT AT THE STROKE OF MIDNIGHT, I WILL HITCH A RIDE TO HEAVEN TO MEET MY MAKER ON THE TAIL OF ACE FREHLEY'S COMET. YOU ARE WELCOME TO JOIN ME.
EH, MAYBE SOME OTHER TIME. BUT IF YOU CHANGE YOUR MIND, WE'LL BE AT MOE'S.

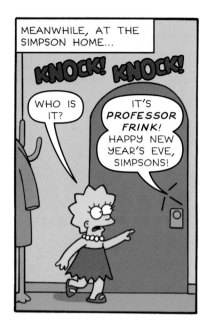

MEANWHILE, AT THE SIMPSON HOME...

KNOCK! KNOCK!

WHO IS IT?

IT'S *PROFESSOR FRINK!* HAPPY NEW YEAR'S EVE, SIMPSONS!

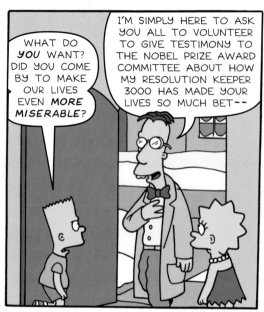

WHAT DO *YOU* WANT? DID YOU COME BY TO MAKE OUR LIVES EVEN *MORE* MISERABLE?

I'M SIMPLY HERE TO ASK YOU ALL TO VOLUNTEER TO GIVE TESTIMONY TO THE NOBEL PRIZE AWARD COMMITTEE ABOUT HOW MY RESOLUTION KEEPER 3000 HAS MADE YOUR LIVES SO MUCH BET--

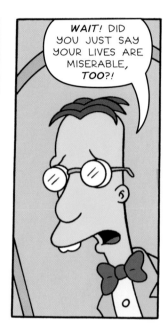

WAIT! DID YOU JUST SAY YOUR LIVES ARE MISERABLE, *TOO?!*

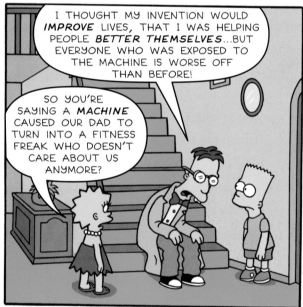

I THOUGHT MY INVENTION WOULD *IMPROVE* LIVES, THAT I WAS HELPING PEOPLE *BETTER THEMSELVES*...BUT EVERYONE WHO WAS EXPOSED TO THE MACHINE IS WORSE OFF THAN BEFORE!

SO YOU'RE SAYING A *MACHINE* CAUSED OUR DAD TO TURN INTO A FITNESS FREAK WHO DOESN'T CARE ABOUT US ANYMORE?

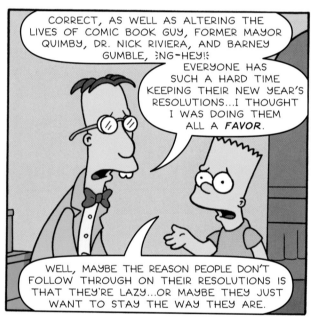

CORRECT, AS WELL AS ALTERING THE LIVES OF COMIC BOOK GUY, FORMER MAYOR QUIMBY, DR. NICK RIVIERA, AND BARNEY GUMBLE, ÐNG-HEY!Ð

EVERYONE HAS SUCH A HARD TIME KEEPING THEIR NEW YEAR'S RESOLUTIONS...I THOUGHT I WAS DOING THEM ALL A *FAVOR*.

WELL, MAYBE THE REASON PEOPLE DON'T FOLLOW THROUGH ON THEIR RESOLUTIONS IS THAT THEY'RE LAZY...OR MAYBE THEY JUST WANT TO STAY THE WAY THEY ARE.

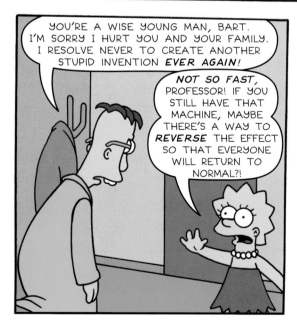

YOU'RE A WISE YOUNG MAN, BART. I'M SORRY I HURT YOU AND YOUR FAMILY. I RESOLVE NEVER TO CREATE ANOTHER STUPID INVENTION *EVER AGAIN!*

NOT SO FAST, PROFESSOR! IF YOU STILL HAVE THAT MACHINE, MAYBE THERE'S A WAY TO *REVERSE* THE EFFECT SO THAT EVERYONE WILL RETURN TO NORMAL?!

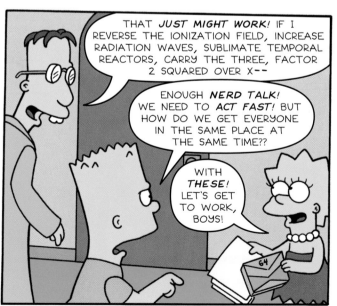

THAT *JUST MIGHT WORK!* IF I REVERSE THE IONIZATION FIELD, INCREASE RADIATION WAVES, SUBLIMATE TEMPORAL REACTORS, CARRY THE THREE, FACTOR 2 SQUARED OVER X--

ENOUGH *NERD TALK!* WE NEED TO *ACT FAST!* BUT HOW DO WE GET EVERYONE IN THE SAME PLACE AT THE SAME TIME??

WITH *THESE!* LET'S GET TO WORK, BOYS!

I HOPE MY FRIENDS AT THE CHURCH OF SCIENTRICKERY LET ME BRING MY AWARD ALONG ON OUR TRIP TONIGHT!
WHAT DO YOU MEAN, YOUR AWARD?!
CONGRATULATIONS. YOU HAVE BEEN CHOSEN AS SPRINGFIELD'S CITIZEN OF THE YEAR. PLEASE COME TO PLANET HYPE TONIGHT TO ACCEPT YOUR AWARD AT MIDNIGHT. CORDIALLY, MAYOR BURNS
I'M THE ONE THEY CHOSE AS CITIZEN OF THE YEAR!
NO, I AM! LOOK, MY INVITATION "CORDIALLY" SAYS SO!
WE HAVE THE EXACT SAME INVITATION, AND UNLESS MY EYES DECEIVE ME, BOTH ARE DRAWN IN FIREHOUSE RED AND BURNT UMBER TONES...STAPLE COLORS OF A 64-COLOR WAXOLA CRAYON BOX!
DOES THAT MEAN WE HAVE TO SHARE THE AWARD?
NO, SIMPLETON, IT MEANS SOMEONE HAS OBVIOUSLY DUPED US INTO COMING HERE WITH THE SAME PROSPECT OF BEING CROWNED WITH SPRINGFIELD'S HIGHEST HONOR!
AND I HAVE A FEELING WE'RE ABOUT TO FIND OUT JUST WHO THAT IS...
NOT YOU TOO!
WHAT IN THE NAME OF ALVAR HANSO IS GOING ON HERE?!
YOU'RE HERE SO WE CAN GIVE YOU BACK YOUR OLD LIVES!

LISA?! ARE YOU SAYING YOU TRICKED US INTO COMING HERE FOR NO GOOD REASON?
WAIT, DOES THIS MEAN I'M NOT WINNING ANY AWARD TONIGHT?
ON THE CONTRARY, DAD... I BROUGHT YOU HERE FOR THE BEST REASON OF ALL! TO REVERSE THE SPELL SCIENCE HAS CAST ON EACH OF YOU THIS PAST YEAR, WHICH HAS MADE ALL OF OUR LIVES WORSE!
YOU SEE, PROFESSOR FRINK EXPOSED YOU ALL TO HIS RESOLUTION KEEPER 3000 LAST NEW YEAR'S EVE, BUT IT DIDN'T CHANGE YOUR LIVES FOR THE BETTER, IT DID THE EXACT OPPOSITE.
GLA-HOVEEN! YOUNG LISA IS CORRECT. NOW, IF YOU ALL JUST STAND STILL FOR A FEW SECONDS, I'LL HAVE YOU BACK TO NORMAL AND HAPPY ONCE MORE.
I DON'T WANT MY OLD LIFE BACK! I'M A REAL DOCTOR NOW WHO TAKES CARE OF EVERY PERSON IN SPRINGFIELD IN THE QUICKEST, CHEAPEST MANNER POSSIBLE!
I CAN CRUSH ACORNS WITH MY TOES! THERE'S NOTHING THAT CAN MAKE ME GIVE THAT UP!
AND I GAVE UP DRINKING TO DONATE EVERY DOLLAR I MAKE TO A CHURCH THAT BELIEVES TROLLS LIVE IN MY MIND AND GIVE ME HEAD-ACHES!
YOU COULDN'T PAY ME TO FORFEIT MY FAITH IN SUCH A ROCK-SOLID ORGANIZATION!
ACTUALLY, I WOULDN'T MIND CHANGING THE EVENTS OF THIS PAST YEAR...
I SECOND THIS...ER, AH...CHUBBY NERD'S SENTIMENT!
WAIT! EVEN IF YOUR LIFE PERSONALLY IS BETTER, IT'S AFFECTED THE LIVES OF PEOPLE AROUND YOU IN A NEGATIVE WAY!

DAD, YOU NEVER SPEND ANY TIME WITH US NOW BECAUSE YOU'RE ALWAYS WORKING OUT OR TRAVELING THE WORLD.
DR. NICK, YOUR PRACTICE HAS BECOME SO POPULAR NO ONE IN SPRINGFIELD CAN ACTUALLY SCHEDULE AN APPOINTMENT AND MORE PEOPLE ARE BEING HURT BY THAT THAN TREATED.
AND BARNEY, YOU'RE GIVING ALL OF YOUR MONEY TO A ***RELIGIOUS GROUP*** THAT MEASURES FAITH BY THE SIZE OF YOUR BANK ACCOUNT!
DON'T YOU UNDERSTAND? YOU DIDN'T NEED TO ***CHANGE*** TO BECOME ***BETTER PEOPLE***...IT'S THE PEOPLE AROUND YOU WHO ***BRING OUT THE BEST*** IN YOU.
HUH. I GUESS WHEN SHE PUTS IT LIKE THAT...
MAYBE WE ***HAVE*** BEEN WRONG THIS PAST YEAR. MAYBE WE WERE ***PERFECT*** JUST THE WAY WE WERE.
NUTS TO THAT! I'M STAYING THIS WAY ***FOREVER!***
KRACK! BLAM! KRUNCH!
NOOOOOOO!!!

LISA...LISA? ...LISA!!
LISA! WAKE UP! IT'S ALMOST MIDNIGHT!
W-WHAT ARE YOU TALKING ABOUT? DIDN'T DAD JUST DESTROY PROFESSOR FRINK'S RESOLUTION MACHINE?
TEN...NINE... EIGHT...SEVEN...
"RESOLUTION MACHINE?!" LIS, PROFESSOR FRINK ISN'T HERE! IT'S NEW YEAR'S EVE, AND YOU FELL ASLEEP!
THEN EVERY-THING'S BACK TO NORMAL! EVERYONE'S STILL LEADING THEIR BORING OLD LIVES?!
SIX...FIVE... FOUR...THREE...
I DON'T KNOW WHAT YOU'RE TALKING ABOUT, BUT YOU MUST'VE HAD SOME CRAZY DREAM!
HERE! GET READY FOR THE TOAST!
TWO... ONE...
HAPPY NEW YEAR!
OH, DAD, I'M SO GLAD YOU'RE STILL YOU! PLEASE DO ME A FAVOR AND NEVER KEEP ANY OF YOUR NEW YEAR'S RESOLUTIONS!
DON'T BE SILLY, HONEY! I NEVER HAVE, AND I NEVER WILL!
THE END

HIBERNATIN' HOMER

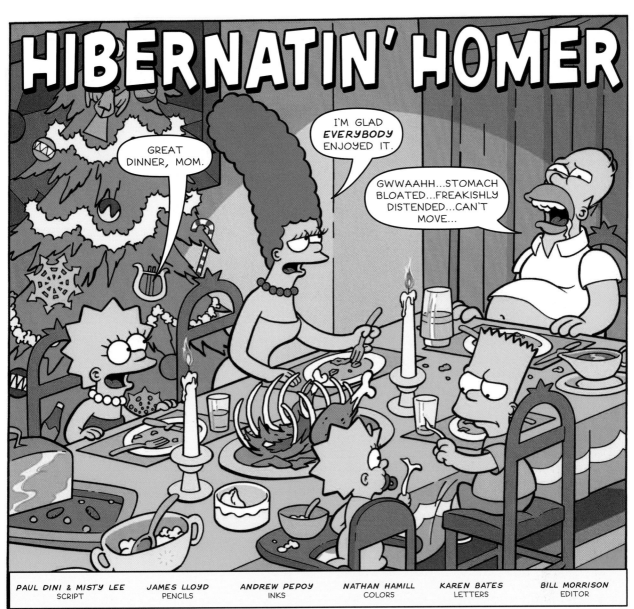

GREAT DINNER, MOM.

I'M GLAD *EVERYBODY* ENJOYED IT.

GWWAAHH...STOMACH BLOATED...FREAKISHLY DISTENDED...CAN'T MOVE...

PAUL DINI & MISTY LEE
SCRIPT

JAMES LLOYD
PENCILS

ANDREW PEPOY
INKS

NATHAN HAMILL
COLORS

KAREN BATES
LETTERS

BILL MORRISON
EDITOR

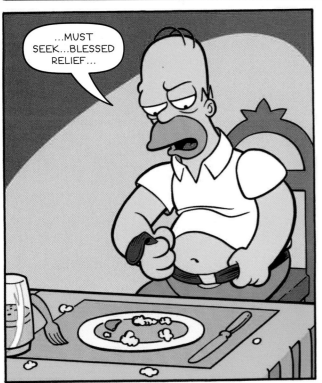

...MUST SEEK...BLESSED RELIEF...

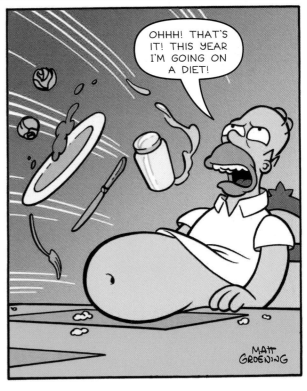

OHHH! THAT'S IT! THIS YEAR I'M GOING ON A DIET!

MATT GROENING

YOU SAY THAT EVERY CHRISTMAS, HOMER.
THIS TIME I MEAN IT!
NO, YOU DON'T!
I THOUGHT YOU'D BE MORE SUPPORTIVE.
NOT WHILE YOU'RE EATING THE LEFTOVER TURKEY BETWEEN TWO PIZZAS!
I CAN'T HELP IT. EVERYTHING IS SO XMAS-LICIOUS!
IT'S TOO BAD YOU CAN'T DIET LIKE A BEAR. THEY LOSE ALMOST FORTY PERCENT OF THEIR BODY WEIGHT BY SLEEPING THROUGH THE WINTER.
UNFORTUNATELY, WE HUMANS ARE STUCK WITH CUTTING CALORIES AND EXERCISING.
SLEEP THROUGH THE WINTER, YOU SAY? HMMM...

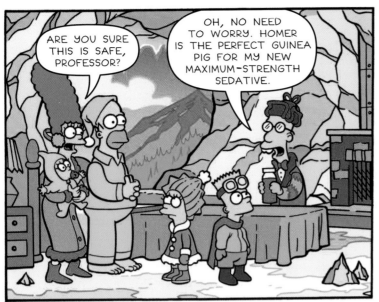

ARE YOU SURE THIS IS SAFE, PROFESSOR?

OH, NO NEED TO WORRY. HOMER IS THE PERFECT GUINEA PIG FOR MY NEW MAXIMUM-STRENGTH SEDATIVE.

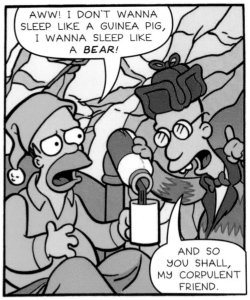

AWW! I DON'T WANNA SLEEP LIKE A GUINEA PIG, I WANNA SLEEP LIKE A *BEAR!*

AND SO YOU SHALL, MY CORPULENT FRIEND.

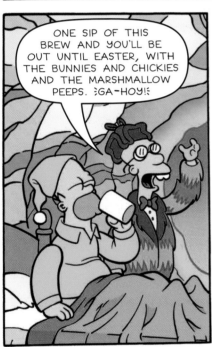

ONE SIP OF THIS BREW AND YOU'LL BE OUT UNTIL EASTER, WITH THE BUNNIES AND CHICKIES AND THE MARSHMALLOW PEEPS. ⋛GA-HOY!⋚

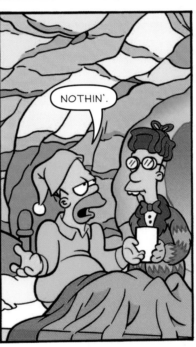

NOTHIN'.

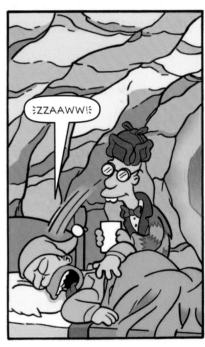

⋛ZZAAWW!⋚

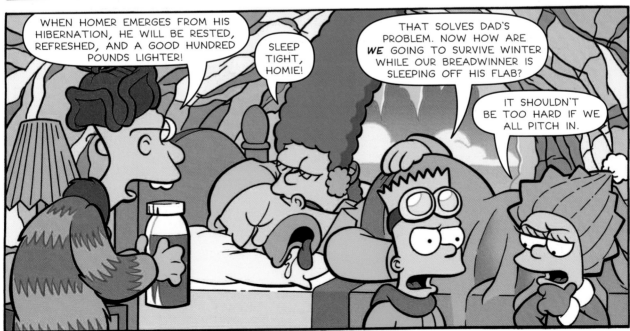

WHEN HOMER EMERGES FROM HIS HIBERNATION, HE WILL BE RESTED, REFRESHED, AND A GOOD HUNDRED POUNDS LIGHTER!

SLEEP TIGHT, HOMIE!

THAT SOLVES DAD'S PROBLEM. NOW HOW ARE *WE* GOING TO SURVIVE WINTER WHILE OUR BREADWINNER IS SLEEPING OFF HIS FLAB?

IT SHOULDN'T BE TOO HARD IF WE ALL PITCH IN.

SIMPSON, EH? I SEEM TO RECALL THE BUTTON-MONKEY IN THIS BOOTH AS A LESS ASSIDUOUS FELLOW.
LARD LAD DONUTS
JANUARY 2ND
BETTER NOW?
CARRY ON.
BUT, MR. BURNS, AS MY REPORT CLEARLY STATES, THE PLANT CAN GO GREEN AND STILL MAKE A PROFIT!
PIE IN THE SKY FLAPADOODLE, SIMPSON. I NEED FACTS I CAN SINK MY TEETH INTO!
JANUARY 10TH
THAT'S MORE LIKE IT, SIMPSON. THESE MARSHED MALLOWED RICE BRICKS ARE DELICIOUS!
JANUARY 17TH
CONGRATULATIONS HOMER
JANUARY 25
EMPLOYEE OF THE MONTH

MEANWHILE, BACK AT THE SNOOZE-CAVE...
ZZZAAWWW...
IN HERE, GENTS...
WE WILL STASH THE GOODS IN THIS OUT-OF-THE-WAY CAVE UNTIL SAINT VALENTINE'S DAY.
BRILLIANT SCHEME, BOSS, HIJACKING ALL THE CONVERSATION HEART SHIPMENTS INTO SPRINGFIELD.
THANK YOU, LEGS. THE LOVEBIRDS WILL HAVE TO PAY DEARLY THIS YEAR IF THEY WANT THEIR "OH U KID."
ZZAWWW...
HEY, WE GOT A SPY!
YOU WANT I SHOULD WASTE SLEEPING UGLY?
NOT SO FAST, LOUIE. THERE IS SOMETHING FAMILIAR ABOUT HIM.
I BELIEVE THIS IS NONE OTHER THAN MY OLD ASSOCIATE IN CRIME, AUGIE "SLEEPY" MANETTI!
THE LEGENDARY SNOOZING HITMAN OF HACKENSACK?!
WE ARE IN THE PRESENCE OF GREATNESS!
NO DOUBT SLEEPY WAS HIDING OUT AFTER A BUSY MONTH OF HOLIDAY WHACKINGS. PERHAPS WE CAN PERSUADE HIM TO JOIN OUR MERRY BAND UNTIL THE SPRING THAW.
ZZAAWWW...
THAT SOUNDS LIKE A YES TO ME.

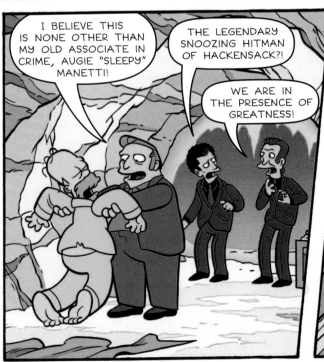

FIX HIM UP NICELY, MARIO. NOTHING IS TOO GOOD FOR SLEEPY MANETTI.
ZZZZ...
SI, SI, FAT TONY.
WELL, HERMAN, I SEE THAT YOU ARE STILL A FEW HUNDRED DOLLARS SHORT ON THOSE AUTHENTIC SICILIAN GARROTES WE OBTAINED FOR YOU.
SORRY, TONY. YOU KNOW HOW IT IS...NO ONE'S SPENDING MONEY AFTER NEW YEAR'S. IF I COULD HAVE ANOTHER COUPLE WEEKS...
I SYMPATHIZE, HERMAN, BUT BUSINESS IS BUSINESS. SLEEPY, LEAN ON HIM.
ZZZZ...
ZZZZ...
OW! I'LL PAY! I'LL PAY!
TO SLEEPY MANETTI! IN THE MONTH SINCE YOU JOINED US, NOT A PAYMENT HAS BEEN MISSED, NOT A DEADBEAT HAS GONE UNFLATTENED!
ZZZ...
TO SLEEPY!
IT CREEPS ME OUT THE WAY HE CAN EAT AND SLEEP LIKE THAT.
THE MAN IS AN ARTIST AT WHAT HE DOES. DO NOT CRITICIZE.
FREEZE, SLEAZE!
TALIA!

IT IS A RAID! GO FOR YOUR PIECE, SLEEPY!
ZZZ... PIECE...
BANG!
BANG!
ZZZ...MMM ...PIECE...!
BANG!
BANG!
BANG!
ZZZZ...
BANG!
FOR OUR ST. PATRICK'S DAY CAMPAIGN WE'LL NEED A QUIRKY CHARACTER TYPE WHO EXUDES ETHNIC CHARM MIXED WITH UNBRIDLED GLUTTONY.
GOOD LUCK! WHERE WOULD WE EVER FIND SUCH A CREATURE?
ZZZZ...
WAIT! WE HAVE A JOB FOR YOU!

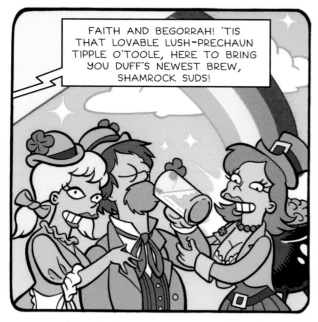

FAITH AND BEGORRAH! 'TIS THAT LOVABLE LUSH-PRECHAUN TIPPLE O'TOOLE, HERE TO BRING YOU DUFF'S NEWEST BREW, SHAMROCK SUDS!

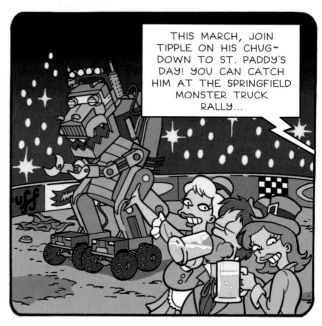

THIS MARCH, JOIN TIPPLE ON HIS CHUG-DOWN TO ST. PADDY'S DAY! YOU CAN CATCH HIM AT THE SPRINGFIELD MONSTER TRUCK RALLY...

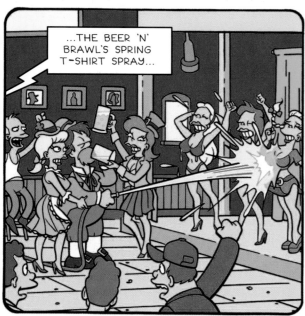

...THE BEER 'N' BRAWL'S SPRING T-SHIRT SPRAY...

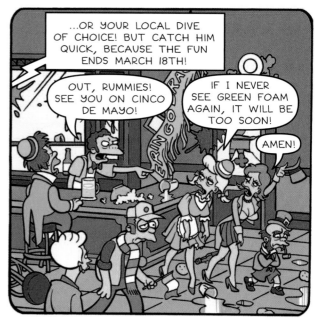

...OR YOUR LOCAL DIVE OF CHOICE! BUT CATCH HIM QUICK, BECAUSE THE FUN ENDS MARCH 18TH!

OUT, RUMMIES! SEE YOU ON CINCO DE MAYO!

IF I NEVER SEE GREEN FOAM AGAIN, IT WILL BE TOO SOON!

AMEN!

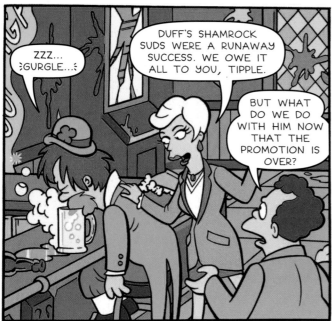

ZZZ... ;GURGLE...;

DUFF'S SHAMROCK SUDS WERE A RUNAWAY SUCCESS. WE OWE IT ALL TO YOU, TIPPLE.

BUT WHAT DO WE DO WITH HIM NOW THAT THE PROMOTION IS OVER?

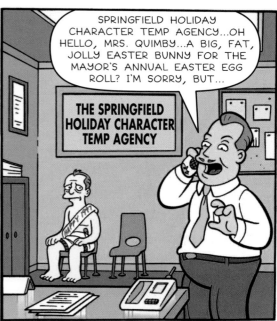

SPRINGFIELD HOLIDAY CHARACTER TEMP AGENCY...OH HELLO, MRS. QUIMBY...A BIG, FAT, JOLLY EASTER BUNNY FOR THE MAYOR'S ANNUAL EASTER EGG ROLL? I'M SORRY, BUT...

THE SPRINGFIELD HOLIDAY CHARACTER TEMP AGENCY

WHY, YEESSSS! WE JUST HAD ONE HOP IN FRESH OFF THE BUNNY TRAIL!
ZZZZAWW...
POSE WITH THE NICE BUNNY, GRETA.
BUT HE'S EATING ALL OUR CANDY!
ROLL THOSE EGGS AND MAKE IT NICE, YOU COTTON-TAILED MORON! WE'VE GOT CRYING CHILDREN HERE!
ZZZZ... ROLL...
WHAAA! ALL THAT'S LEFT OF MY CANDY LAMB IS HIS EYES!
YOU'RE A PIGGIE, SANTA CLAUS!
ZZZZ... ROLL...
ZZZZZ... ROLL...
ZZZ... WHEEE!

ZZZZ... OW...OW...
ZZZZ...
ACCORDING TO MY CALCULATIONS, YOUR FATHER SHOULD BE EMERGING FROM HIBERNATION RIGHT ABOUT...NOW!
RISE AND SHINE, HOMER.
ZZZ...HUH?
HOW DO YOU FEEL?
HUNGRY.
HOW MUCH WEIGHT DID HE SLEEP OFF, PROFESSOR?
OH MY GLAVIN! THIS IS INCREDIBLE!
NOT ONLY HAS HOMER RETAINED HIS ENTIRE BODY FAT CONTENT, BUT HE'S ALSO GAINED FIFTY-SIX POUNDS!
WHAT?!?
YOU, SIR, ARE A TRUE MIRACLE OF SCIENCE!
WOOO-HOO!
THE END

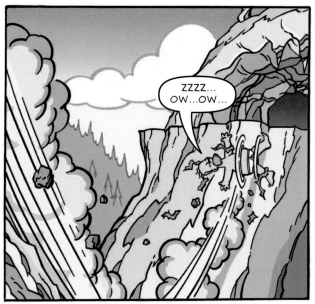